MODERN AMERICAN ARMOR

Below: M109 self-propelled 155mm howitzers take-up positions near Riedenheim during the 'Reforger IV' exercises in Germany, 1973. These vehicles are from Battery C, 2/33rd Artillery, and have been given a coat of temporary camouflage, probably either mud or a washable tempera paint. (US Army)

Below: M109 self-propelled 155mm howitzers take-up positions near Riedenheim during the 'Reforger IV' exercises in Germany, 1973. These vehicles are from Battery C, 2/33rd Artillery, and have been given a coat of temporary camouflage, probably either mud or a washable tempera paint. (US Army)

MODERN AMERICAN ARMOR

Combat Vehicles of the United States Army Today
Steven J. Zaloga and Lt.-Col. James W. Loop

a&
ap

Arms & Armour Press
London-Melbourne-Harrisburg, Pa.

Glossary

Abbreviation	Full term	Abbreviation	Full term
AA	Anti-aircraft	HIMAG	High Mobility Agility
AAI	AAI Corporation, formerly Aircraft Armament Inc., but full name no longer used	HMWC	High Mobility Weapons Carrier
		HSTV-L	High Survivability Test Vehicle – Light
AAV	Airborne Assault Vehicle	IAFV	Infantry Armoured Fighting Vehicle
ACAV	Armoured Car Assault Vehicle	IFF	Identification, Friend or Foe
ACCV	Armoured Cavalry Cannon Vehicle	IFV	Infantry Fighting Vehicle
ACVT	Armoured Combat Test Vehicle	IR	Infra-Red
AIFS	Advanced Infra-red Seeker	ISU	Integrated Sight Unit
AIFV	Advanced Infantry Fighting Vehicle	ITV	Improved Tow Vehicle
AM	American Motors Corporation	LAV	Light Armoured Vehicle
AmTrac	Amphibious Tractor	LAW	Light Anti-Tank Weapon
AOS	Add-On Stabilization. Gun stabilization system	LAWCV	Light Armoured Wheeled Combat Vehicle
AP	Armour Piercing	LLLTV	Low Light Level Television
APDS	Armour Piercing, Discarding Sabot	LVA	Landing Vehicle Assault
APG	Aberdeen Proving Grounds, Aberdeen, Maryland	LVT	Landing Vehicle Tracked
APHE	Armour Piercing, High Explosive	LVTE	Landing Vehicle Tracked, Engineer
AR	Armoured Reconnaissance	LVTH	Landing Vehicle Tracked, Howitzer
ARSV	Armoured Reconnaissance Scout Vehicle	LVTP	Landing Vehicle Tracked, Personnel
ARVN	Army of the Republic of Vietnam	LVTR	Landing Vehicle Tracked, Recovery
AT	Anti-Tank	MAC	Medium Armoured Car
ATAC	Army Tank and Automotive Command (currently US Army Tank and Automotive Research and Development Command, Warren, Michigan)	MBU	Mobile Test Unit
		MERDC	Mobility Equipment Research and Development (Command)
BMY	Bowen–McLoughlin–York Corporation	MICV	Mechanized Infantry Combat Vehicle
CBR	Chemical, Biological, Radiological (also called NBC, Nuclear, Biological, Chemical or ABC, Atomic, Biological, Chemical)	MLRS	Multiple Launcher Rocket System
		MPG	Mobile Protected Gun
		MPWS	Mobile Protected Weapon System
CEV	Combat Engineer Vehicle	MTBF	Mean Time Between Failures
CFV	Cavalry Fighting Vehicle	ND:YAG	Neodymium: Yttrium Aluminium Garnet. The crystal used in a type of solid-state laser which gives it its particular waverlength (1.06 microns)
CSV	Combat Support Vehicle		
DDAD	Detroit Diesel Allison Division (General Motors)		
DIVAD	Divisional Air Defence		
DSWS	Divisional Support Weapon System	OPFOR	Opposing Forces
DU	Depleted Uranium	OPTRAC	Optical Tracking. Light beam rangefinder system
ENTAC	Engin Teléguidé Anti-Char. First generation, wire-guided missile	PACCAR	Pacific Car and Foundry Corporation
		PIP	Product Improvement Programme
FAAR	Forward Area Alerting Radar	PIVAD	Product Improved Vulcan Air Defence
FIST	Fire Support Team Vehicle	PLRS	Position Location Reporting System
FLASH	XM191 multi-shot flame-throwing weapon	RAP	Rocket Assisted Projectiles
FLIR	Forward Looking Infra-Red	SLEP	Service Life Extension Programme
Frag-HE	Fragmentation-High Explosive	SPAT	Self-Propelled Anti-Tank gun
FVS	Fighting Vehicle Systems	TAC	Tactical Air Control
GLAAD	Gun Low Altitude Air Defence	TBAT	TOW-Bushmaster Armoured Turret
GSRS	General Support Rocket System	TC	Tank Commander
HE	High Explosive	TOW	Tube-launched, Optically-tracked, Wire-guided. A heavy wire-guided anti-tank missile
HEAT	High Explosive, Anti-Tank		
HELBAT	Human Engineering Laboratory Battalion Artillery Tests	TOWCAP	TOW Covered Armour Protection
		TRTG	Tactical Radar Threat Generator
HERA	High Explosive, Rocket-Assisted	TTS	Tank Thermal Sight. Passive night sight for tanks
HVAP	High Velocity Armour Piercing	UV	Ultra Violet

Contents

To my wife, Margie, who was so understanding during my research for this book, and my daughters Janet, Karen, Laura and Susan, in the hopes they will be spared another war in their lifetime — J.W.L.

Published by
Arms and Armour Press,
Lionel Leventhal Limited.

Great Britain:
2 – 6 Hampstead High Street,
London NW3 1QQ

Australia:
4 – 12 Tattersalls Lane,
Melbourne, Victoria 3000.

United States of America:
Cameron and Kelker Streets,
P.O. Box 1831, Harrisburg,
Pa. 17105

© Lionel Leventhal Limited, 1982
All rights reserved. No part of this publication may be reproduced, stored in a retrieval system, or transmitted in any form by any means electrical, mechanical or otherwise, without first seeking the written permission of the copyright owner and of the publisher.

British Library Cataloguing in Publication Data:
Zaloga, Steven J.
Modern American Armour
1. Armoured Vehicles, Military — United States
I. Title II. Loop, James W.
623. 74'75'0973 UG446.5
ISBN 0-85368-248-8
Edited by Tessa Rose.
Designed by Anthony A. Evans.
Typeset by Typesetters (Birmingham) Limited.
Printed and bound by William Clowes (Beccles) Limited.

Below: An M163 Vulcan of the 2nd Armored Division scans the sky over the town of Feuchtwangen, Germany. (US Army)

Note on data tables: A dash indicates that no data is required because it is not relevant to that particular vehicle. A blank indicates that the data is not available.

Preface

The United States Army had a tank force smaller than that of Poland at the outset of the Second World War in 1939. By the time America entered the war two years later, its heavy industry had begun to gear up for war production and by 1945 had manufactured about 287,000 armoured vehicles, more than any other nation during the war. American tanks and armoured vehicles formed the backbone of nearly every Allied armoured force except that of the Soviet Union. Similarly, for nearly two decades after the war, the United States was the principal source of armoured vehicles for NATO, with only Britain being relatively self-sufficient in this area. By the 1960s this began to change; France and Germany began to manufacture main battle tanks. France and Britain had considerable success in exporting their vehicles to Third World countries, which had previously relied exclusively on the United States. These countries began to challenge American technical hegemony in NATO, though US designs especially in the area of self-propelled guns and armoured troop carriers remained very popular. Besides the general resurgence in European heavy industry, the troubled state of American tank development in the 1960s was another factor in this trend away from American technical dominance in armoured vehicles. The US Army embarked on a series of overly ambitious and highly sophisticated armoured vehicles such as the MBT – 70, M551, Mauler and Vigilante, most of which withered on the vine because of insoluble technical problems, excessive complexity, unrealistic costs and the general paucity of research funds due to the escalating cost of the Vietnam War. As a result, in the early 1970s the US Army remained equipped with armoured vehicles over a decade old in design with no replacements available in the foreseeable future. Most of the existing vehicles were sound and effective designs that could be enhanced by modification programmes, but the lag in armoured vehicle development coincided with a major surge in Soviet armoured vehicle development. The Warsaw Pact had long enjoyed a numerical edge over NATO but this was blunted by the technical advantages enjoyed by the armoured vehicles of NATO. The Soviet Union's new family of armoured vehicles, including the T – 62 combat tank, BMP infantry combat vehicle, ZSU – 23 – 4 Shilka air defence gun vehicle, and SA – 6 air defence missile vehicle, challenged this technological lead and these vehicles were manufactured in sizeable quantities.

The US response was a multi-faceted effort to maintain the conventional balance of forces in Europe. The US Army has never attempted to match the Soviet Army tank for tank but has relied over the past decades on a triad of tactical air power, high-quality anti-tank missiles and a smaller, but better trained and equipped tank force. A new armoured vehicle programme embarked upon in the early 1970s is only now reaching fruition, with the first vehicles of the new generation beginning to enter service units. The new designs, such as the M1 Abrams, M2 Bradley, M3 Devers and MLRS, were developed with less emphasis on the sort of extravagant technical ingenuity that poisoned many of the projects of the 1960s, and more emphasis was placed on proven technological advances. Since the 1960s, there have been many important break-throughs in armour design, radar and laser fire control systems, advanced ammunition and night vision which have enabled the Army to realize the goals first set in the 1960s, but without pushing the projects to the precarious brink of unproven technologies. Many of the new designs have attracted a great deal of critical attention, especially the M1 Abrams. This has been due not so much to any particularly severe teething problems but to heightened Congressional scrutiny after the failures of the 1960s which has tended to amplify their criticism. While the new generation of designs are unlikely to restore the dominance American armoured vehicles once enjoyed, they will reinstate their hard-earned reputation for reliable, well balanced designs, and make an important stride in keeping American units a step ahead of the Soviets.

This book is a companion volume to the earlier book *Modern Soviet Armour.* In distinct contrast to the earlier study, where even the barest facts were difficult to obtain, in the case of American armoured vehicle development there is simply so much material available that it becomes very difficult to decide what a modest overview such as this should contain. The aim has been to concentrate on vehicles that actually entered service use, though important developmental efforts and designs earmarked for foreign export are also covered, and the scope of the book has also been carefully restricted to tactical armoured combat vehicles. As the title implies, special emphasis is given to current vehicle types and those on the verge of entering service use. The scale drawings included are all to a constant 1/76 scale.

The authors have been privileged to receive the assistance of dozens of specialists in the field while preparing this book. Nevertheless, the statements and opinions put forth are solely those of the authors and do not represent the views of any agencies of the US Army or any of the defence firms consulted. Our thanks go to Leland Ness for help on many technical matters; Brian Gibbs, formerly a tanker and photographer with the 73rd Armor for providing many of the fine photographs; Midic Castelletti, photographer with the 50th Armored Division for other photographs; Colonel R. J. Icks (AUS, retd.) for his generous support over the years; George Balin, for his photographs of US armour in foreign service and other help; George Woodard for his photographs from Fort Knox; David Holmes for material on the M2/M3 programme; Peter Frandsen for research in the National Archives; and to Robert M. McDonald for research in Detroit. We would also like to thank the following individuals and organizations for their generous response to our inquiries: Captain Russell Vaughan, US Army; Major Frederick W. Crismon, US Army; John A. Loop; Lieutenant Colonel John Sloan, US Army (retd.); Mrs. Marie Yates, US Army Audio-Visual Agency; Captain Edwin W. Besch, USMC (retd.); Donald R. Warner; Captain Terrill M. Aitken, ORARNG; William F. Murray; J. Tyler Segar; William Auerbach; Joseph Meheuran; US Army Audio Visual Agency – Still Photographic Library; US Army Armament Research & Development Command – DIVAD Programme Office; US Army Tank & Automotive Material Readiness Command – Major Don Bullock (XMI Project Office); Lieutenant Colonel Alexander (M60A3 Project Office); M113 Project Office; M551 Project Office; Lieutenant Colonel David Doyle (FVS Project Office, West Coast); US Marine Corps Headquarters, Historical Branch and Photo Archives; US Navy Sea Systems Command; AAI Corporation; Ares, Inc.; Arrowpointe Corp.; Boeing Aerospace Company; Bowen – McLaughlin – York Corporation (BMY); Thomas Jambriska, Cadillac Gage Corporation; Chrysler Corporation Defense Group; Emerson Electronics & Space Division; Food Machinery Corporation (FMC) – R. B. Foss (FVS systems); Charles Lieb (M113 programmes); Ford Aerospace & Communications Corporation; General Dynamics, Pomona Division; Hughes Missile Systems Group; R. Goodwin, Raytheon Company.

Steven J. Zaloga and James W. Loop, 1981.

Left: The Sherman tank remained in US Army service throughout the Korean War, but was supplanted in the armoured divisions by the newer M26 Pershing and its successors. Nevertheless, the Sherman lingered on in other armies, serving with great distinction with Israeli troops in the 1956, 1967 and 1973 wars. This pair of M4A1 (76mm) are taking part in summer manoeuvres in the Sinai in 1961. They are prominently marked with large tactical insignia to avoid the confusion caused during the 1956 fighting when Israeli tanks were without unit insignia. (Israeli Defence Force)
Right: Gaudily painted M46 Patton tanks of the 6th Tank Battalion take-up positions near Yangpung on 7 March 1951 during the fighting in Korea. The M46 closely resembled the earlier M26 but had an improved engine. It is externally distinguishable from the M26 by the exhaust silencers on the rear of the mudguards. Several US tank battalions in Korea painted their tanks with dragon and tiger faces in a curious attempt to frighten Chinese troops. (US Army)

Battle Tanks

At the conclusion of the Second World War, the US Army fielded an impressive armada of tanks, ranging from the M5A1 Stuart and M24 Chaffee light tanks to the ubiquitous M4 Sherman medium tank and the M26 Pershing heavy tank. By 1945, the M5A1 Stuart was clearly obsolete and was mustered out to end its days in foreign service or in a scrap-yard. It was replaced by the M24 Chaffee, which had begun to enter service in the winter of 1944. The Sherman was the most widely-produced American tank of the war, and was the backbone of the armoured divisions of the US, British, French, Commonwealth and Free Polish armies throughout the later years of the fighting. However, it was not an unqualified success, particularly when faced by the heavier German Panther in late 1944 and 1945. Its main guns, both the earlier short 75mm and later long 76mm gun, were inadequate to penetrate the thick frontal armour of the Panther or Royal Tiger, and its armour did not compare to that of its opponents. This situation had arisen out of the greater priority the US Army placed on high levels of tank production and vehicle reliability, on the doctrine of Army Ground Forces headed by Lieutenant General Lesley McNair, and on complacency over German tank design. McNair felt that the principal rôle of armoured divisions should be rapid exploitation, and that the Sherman's reliability, speed and availability served this task better than a more heavily-armoured and armed tank that would be ready too late and in too small a quantity. He felt that the business of repulsing enemy armour should be left to the more heavily-armed tank destroyers. The tank destroyer concept did not live up to expectations and the Tank Destroyer Command was abolished after the war. The combined team of tanks, mechanized infantry, mechanized artillery and air support proved very able in dealing with German armour, and the Sherman's virtues appropriate to the hell-for-leather drives through France and Germany. Still, the mediocre performance of American tanks against the Panther remained bitterly etched in the memories of American tank commanders after the war and led to great interest in heavy firepower and long-range fire capability.

The M26 Pershing Heavy Tank. During the last months of the war in Europe, a handful of new M26 Pershings entered combat in Germany. The M26 was called a heavy tank at the time but was, in fact, in the same size and weight class as the German Panther medium tank. It was far more able to deal with the Panther or Tiger tank than the Sherman, and after 1945 gradually began replacing those M4A3E8s still in service. The Sherman lingered on into the 1950s, mainly in the National Guard, but it did serve with distinction in the Korean War. It was widely supplied overseas, and still soldiers on in some smaller armies. Modified and upgunned versions performed very well in Israeli hands in all the Arab-Israeli wars.

American tank development slowed considerably after the war. The only major programmes were a series of heavy tank studies initiated in 1944 with the monstrous Royal Tiger in mind. These tanks, the T29, T30 and T34, were very heavily armed (with 105mm, 155mm and 120mm guns respectively) but never entered production. The meagre resources available to Army Tank and Automotive Command (ATAC) were spent on more prosaic studies of basic tank technology, such as track, engine and transmission design. A new trio of tanks was begun in 1949 and 1950, just before the onset of the Korean War.

Korea shook the Army out of its lethargy. The initial North Korean attacks were spearheaded by T – 34 – 85 tanks supplied by the Soviet Union, and these quickly cut through the poorly equipped South Korean and American forces. Small numbers of light M24s did little to help, and it was not until the arrival of M4A3E8s, M26 Pershings and fighter-bombers that the North Korean tanks were contained. The Shermans and Pershings proved very able to deal with the T – 34, and the North Koreans and Chinese were very reluctant to waste their tanks in encounters with the better-trained American crews. The M26s were eventually replaced by M46 Patton tanks. The M46 was a rebuilt derivative of the M26, first developed in 1948. The troublesome engine and transmission in the M26 was replaced, a bore evacuator was added to the gun and improvements made to the gun fire control system and the suspension. Externally, the M26 and M46 were very similar except for the changes on the gun (later added to the M26 to result in the M26A1) and in the engine deck area. There were very few M26 or M46 exported outside the United States to other armies.

The important rôle played by North Korean tanks in the early part of the Korean War focused attention on the poor shape of the US tank force and catalyzed a new tank development effort. The 1949 trio of interrelated tanks consisted of the T41 light tank, the T42 medium tank and the T43 heavy tank. They shared many common components in the hopes of simplifying logistical requirements during wartime, but none was suitable for production in time for use in Korea. The T41 would eventually enter service as the M41 Walker Bulldog light tank; its development is covered here in the section on cavalry vehicles.

The M103 Heavy Tank. The T43 heavy tank was rushed into production in 1950 in the hysteria after the initial North Korean tank successes. The first vehicles of an eventual batch of 200 tanks were ready in 1952, and the type was accepted for Army use as the M103 heavy tank. The M103 was the largest tank ever adopted by the US Army and mounted an impressive 120mm gun, aimed with the use of a sophisticated and costly stereoscopic rangefinder. The M103, which had been designed with the memory of the German Royal Tiger in mind, was intended for long-range tank duels and to counter the Soviet IS – 3 and T – 10 heavy tanks. Two loaders were needed to handle its enormous rounds, and it was thickly armoured. It was a sluggish vehicle (although the chassis was little more than a stretched medium tank chassis) and did not bear up well under its considerable weight. It had phenomenal fuel consumption and many teething pains due to the haste with which it was rushed into production. Basic modifications were required to the suspension, engine and fire controls. These modifications resulted in the M103A1, beginning in 1954. Two M103A1 battalions, each with sixty-nine tanks, served with the 1st and 2nd Armored Divisions in Germany and several companies were supplied to the Marines. The threat of the IS – 3 and T – 10 had been greatly exaggerated, as was evident when several IS – 3s were inspected in the aftermath of the 1956 Arab-Israeli War.

Newer medium tank designs were capable of carrying out the duties of these overrated tanks, and in 1958 when the armoured divisions switched over to the pentomic formation, the heavy tank battalion was dropped. The remaining M103A1s were turned over to the Marines, whose meagre budget made them happy to receive any scraps from the Army's table. In 1962 another modernization effort was initiated, replacing the engine with an AVDS 1790 diesel similar to that used in the M60. A total of 153 vehicles were modified. They entered Marine service as the M103A2, where they remained for nearly a

decade. The Army experimented with several heavy tank designs in the later 1950s, but the increasing firepower of medium tanks (or main battle tanks as they became known) rendered these efforts redundant and none was produced for Army use.

The M47 Medium Tank. The last member of the 1949 trio, the T42, never materialized in active service. It proved to be under-engined, but its turret — with a sophisticated stereoscopic rangefinder similar to that on the M103 — offered better long-range gun performance and better ballistic protection than the turret on the M46. Attempts to mate the T42 turret with an M46 hull resulted in the M47 medium tank. The M47 incorporated a number of modifications on the hull. It was rushed into production, with the first machines leaving the assembly lines in 1951. Serious flaws in the complicated fire control system, aggravated by the haste in which the M47 was placed into quantity production, led to the vehicles being sidelined until the problems could be resolved. The stereoscopic rangefinder never lived-up to expectations; in no small measure due to the great skill required to operate it correctly. The M47 never saw combat in US hands, and its tenure in US Army service was unremarkable and short-lived due to the rapid introduction of the superior M48 Patton. Nevertheless, the M47 played a vital rôle in the growth of the NATO tank force. It was the first modern tank to be made available for export to NATO after the Second World War, and formed the backbone of most of the NATO tank units well into the 1960s. Of the 9,100 produced, over 8,500 were exported where they served in large numbers with the French, West German, Italian, Greek and Turkish armies. The M47 made its combat début during 1956 when tanks of the French 8e Dragons were landed at Port Said during the Suez Canal operation. It experienced its first taste of heavy fighting with the Pakistani Army in the war with India in 1965. It also served with the Royal Jordanian Armour Corps against Israel in 1967, in 1974 with the Turkish Army in the invasion of Cyprus, and in 1977 with the Ethiopian Army in the Ogaden war. It has not been one of the more highly acclaimed tanks of its generation, though this can be blamed as much on its crews in combat as on any inherent flaws in the vehicle itself. Many M47s remain in service, and there have been numerous attempts to modernize and up-arm it. The two most notable programmes were the efforts by Chrysler España to re-engine it with an AVDS 1790 diesel for the Spanish Army, resulting in the new M47S, and the BMY programme in Iran to modernize the M47s of Iran, Pakistan, Jordan and other Muslim states in the region. The Iranian revolution in 1979 cut short these plans, though the M47s of Iran and Pakistan were brought up to M47M standards through the addition of an AVDS 1790 diesel engine and new Cadillac Gage turret fire control improvements.

The M48 Patton Medium Tank. The M47 had been rushed into production in 1951 due to the deplorable shape of the American tank force. It was really only an interim solution to the problem and, in the meantime, a more satisfactory vehicle, the M48, was designed. The M48 represented a far more drastic re-working of the basic M46 design, as it incorporated a new armour layout for the hull and turret and a spate of automotive improvements. It featured a well designed hemispherical turret with excellent ballistic protection, and a distinctive boat-shaped bow. The M48 was also the first American medium tank to dispense with the fifth crewman. The fifth crewman had served as a co-driver, radio operator and hull machine-gun operator, but his space could be filled better with ammunition, and his tasks taken over by other crew members or eliminated. The troublesome stereoscopic range-finder was retained, and it was not until the M48A3 that a simpler coincidence rangefinder was adopted. Nevertheless, the stereoscopic rangefinder offered excellent long-range accuracy if used properly. While a Sherman tank using a ballistic reticle rangefinder had about a five per cent probability of a first-round hit at a range of 1,500m, on the M48 the probability was nearly fifty per cent, if used properly. The first pilot models of the new Patton were

M47 Patton medium tank

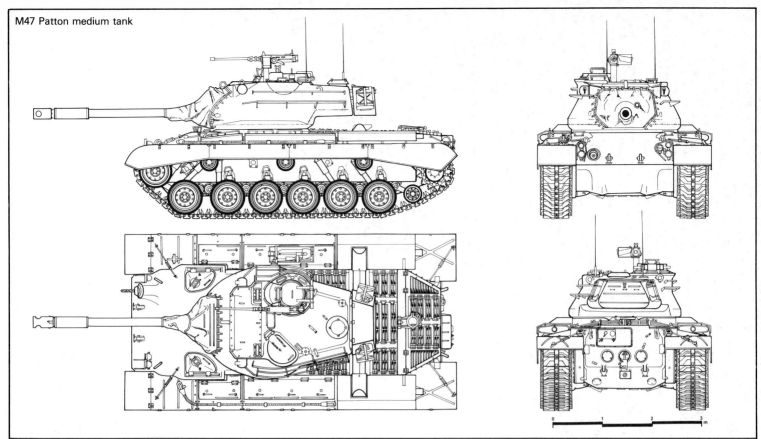

Left, top: The M103 heavy tank was the companion to the Patton medium tanks. It was designed to provide long-range firepower and to deal with Soviet heavy tanks. Although very thickly armoured, it was sluggish and the Army gladly turned over its M103s to the Marines in the late 1950s. This M103A1 of the 3rd Armored Division at Grafenwöhr, Germany, in 1959 was one of the last M103s in Army service. (US Army)

Left, middle: An M47 Patton tank of the 57th Tank Battalion, 2nd Armored Division, during Operation 'Monte Carlo' in Germany, 1953. The M47 was the first thoroughly new medium tank introduced into the US Army after the Second World War. The main improvement over previous types was its sophisticated, albeit troublesome, stereoscopic rangefinder, which gave the tank much better accuracy at longer ranges. The right-hand side viewing port for the rangefinder, a small hemispheric dome, can be seen. (US Army)

Left, below: The M47's service life in the US Army was brief, owing to shortcomings in the design and the rapid arrival of its successor, the M48 Patton, which used an improved turret. The M47s were transferred in large numbers to allied armies in NATO and the Middle East. In the late 1970s several of the Muslim countries using the M47 decided to modernize their tanks with the addition of a diesel engine similar to that used on the M60, and new fire controls. This version was called the M47M, and the vehicles were re-manufactured at a plant in Iran set up by the American firm BMY. The Iranian revolution put paid to this venture and only Pakistan's M47s were modified to the improved configuration (shown here). (BMY)

Right, top: The M48 bore a close family resemblance to earlier members of the Patton series, especially in regards to the basic chassis, but adopted a better, shaped hemispherical turret, a boat-shaped bow, and engine and automotive improvements. The initial version had an exposed machine-gun over the commander's hatch, but the M48A2 (pictured here) used a prominent M1 machine-gun cupola that allowed the weapon to be fired from inside the tank. This Patton of the 3/40th Armored, 1st Cavalry Division, patrols along a ridge in Korea during 1962. The triangular tactical insignia indicates Company A. The vehicle has been given a coat of improvized mud camouflage. (US Army)

Right, below: The distinctive feature of the M48 and M48A1, compared to subsequent versions of the M48 family, was its low engine deck with a profusion of exhaust and intake grilles. This M48A1 of the 4/69th Armor is taking machine-gun practice at Fort Benning, Georgia, 1964. (US Army)

completed in December 1951, and the production models entered service in 1953. The initial M48s were hurried into production with the design work on several features incomplete. As a result, the first production model used a simple low-profile tank commander's (TC) hatch with an externally mounted .50 calibre machine-gun. The delayed improvements were incorporated shortly afterwards on the M48A1, which can be most easily distinguished by its prominent M1 TC cupola. This cupola is, in fact, a sub-turret armed with a .50 calibre machine-gun for use against troops and low-flying aircraft. It has been widely criticized from some quarters as adding unnecessarily to the height and weight of the vehicle while at the same time distracting the commander from his primary rôle of directing the crew. Nonetheless, it has remained a trademark of American tanks to this day.

The M48 and M48A1, like the M47 and M103, were also victims of the rush to build-up American tank strength in the wake of the Korean War. Both vehicles were plagued by teething problems that required costly rebuilding efforts. Once these problems were overcome, the M48 Patton proved a robust and effective tank. It suffered from appallingly short range — only 70 miles without external fuel tanks — in common with most tanks of its generation. In 1955 an improved fuel-injection engine was designed, resulting in the M48A2. This model combined greater internal fuel stowage and increased fuel efficiency and doubled the tank's cruising range to 160 miles. A new, raised engine deck was added to provide better engine cooling. A sub-variant of this version was the M48A2C, which had fire control and vision improvements. The only external difference between these models was the deletion of a small idler wheel at the rear of the suspension between the drive sprocket and end road wheel. The M48A2 finally ironed-out the problems that had plagued its elder siblings. The M48 first saw combat in 1965 with the Pakistani Army. In the 1967 war in the Middle East, M48s were used by the Royal Jordanian Armour Corps while the Israelis used M48A2Cs. During the fighting in Sinai, there were many encounters between the Pattons and Soviet T–55s and in the hands of skilled Israeli tankers the Pattons almost invariably came out on top. The M48A2 was exported in modest numbers, the largest foreign user being the Bundeswehr. The first M48A2s entered Army service in 1956 and were subsequently adopted by the US Marine Corps.

Although the Army was content with the M48 Patton series, various attempts were made to develop a more effective replacement. Newer and larger tank guns had heavier and more awkward rounds that were difficult for a single crewman to lift and chamber. It was felt that these problems could be circumvented by designing an automatic loader, which would also open up prospects of increased rates of fire. Various attempts to develop such a system for conventional turrets were unsuccessful, as the results were invariably too complicated, too heavy or too large. The French pioneered a novel approach to the problem in the form of oscillating turrets. These turrets resembled a universal joint. The turret proper was mounted on a trunnion platform to provide elevation, and the trunnion platform provided traverse by means of a conventional turret race. The main gun could then be mounted in a stationary position in the turret, since the entire turret moved in elevation. This permitted the designers to develop much smaller auto-loaders to fit conveniently into the turret bustle. The Army investigated a family of oscillating turret tanks, including the T69 (with a 90mm gun), the T54 (with a 105mm gun) and the T77 (with a 120mm gun). The prototypes of the T69 and T54 entered trials in 1955 and 1956, but their advantages were far outweighed by their disadvantages, notably their weight, complexity and armour protection.

When M60A1 production was well underway, the Army decided to re-engine some of its M48A1s and A2s with the same power plant and rear engine deck, resulting in the M48A3. The M48A2 and M48A3 are quite similar externally, but can be distinguished from one another by the presence of the air filter box on the mudguard of the M48A3.

Left, top: The M48A2 incorporated automotive improvements over the M48A1 and finally worked out the problems painfully evident in its elder siblings. A new raised engine deck, fitted to cut down on infra-red emissions, is the distinctive feature of this version. This M48A2 was photographed in Vietnam in 1968. (James Loop)

Left, middle: Several attempts were made to develop a heavy tank fitted with an automatic loader for the main gun. One approach to this problem was the development of oscillating turrets, in which the whole core of the turret elevates, not just the gun. The T54 was one of the experimental tanks used to investigate this technique. Although the French successfully used the method on their AMX – 13, it was never used on a tank adopted for US Army service. (S. Zaloga)

Left, below: The M48A3 was nearly identical externally to the M48A2, but its new diesel engine offered significant improvements in range and fuel economy, and was preferred in Vietnam. This view of a Marine M48A3 clearly shows the changes on the rear deck, most notably the large rectangular air-filter boxes mounted centrally on either track-guard. (USMC)

Top: The M48A2 was the mainstay of the Bundeswehr tank force until the advent of the Leopard in the early 1960s. Some of its M48A2Cs were supplied to Israel in 1965, while many of the remainder were later upgunned with a 105mm gun in the late 1970s and called the M48A2GA2. These M48A2Cs of the West German Panzer Abteilung 200 are taking part in the 1973 'Reforger IV' NATO exercises near Bernsfeld. (US Army)

Middle: Although the M48A3 proved quite able to absorb heavy battlefield damage, including multiple RPG – 7 anti-tank rocket hits, Pattons on convoy patrol duty were sometimes reinforced with sandbags to protect their crews. In sweltering heat they often preferred to fight outside the turret, like this crew from the 3/4th Cavalry, 1968. (James Loop)

Right: M48A3s in Vietnam were usually fitted with G350 turret riser blocks, which offered better all-round vision from the commander's position. This Patton of Company B, 1/77th Armor, taking part in a sweep near Fire Base 2 near Cam Lo in July 1970, has this feature, and is bedecked with an assortment of supply and ammunition containers for carrying the crew's personal stores. (US Army)

race and the idea was dropped. The T95E2 was a low-risk version using an M48 turret with a 90mm gun to serve as a back-up should the other armaments fail. Subsequently, this vehicle was used as a test bed to adapt the 105mm gun to the M48. The T95E3 was armed with a 105mm smoothbore, and the T95E6 was armed with an even larger 120mm smoothbore. The first prototypes were ready in 1958 and put through their trials. Some of the technologies on which the T95 was based were not mature enough and caused endless delays and problems. For example, the OPTRAC system, which was a forerunner of later laser rangefinders, proved delicate and frequently inaccurate. Congress was critical of both the complexity and cost of the vehicle and anxious over the prospect of a new battle tank likely to suffer from the same teething pains experienced in the M47/M48 Patton programme. The adoption of the T95 would have required a complete re-tooling of the tank factories, substantially adding to the cost of the vehicle, and, for these reasons, the Army decided to terminate the project in favour of a modernized M48. The T95 continued to serve as an important test bed for new automotive and armament technologies. It was the first American tank to be experimentally fitted with the new composite armours being developed.

The M60 and M60A1 Main Battle Tanks. In 1956, British Intelligence acquired precise information about the armour on the new T-54 Soviet tank. The British Army felt it prudent to develop a new tank gun more adequate to handle this thickly armoured opponent. During the armament trials of the T95, this weapon, the L7 105mm rifled tank gun, was examined by the US Army and found to be superior to other available and experimental tank weapons. After redesigning the breech, the United States decided to use it in their own tanks as the M68 105mm gun. It was successfully fitted into an M48A2 turret, but further improvements to the vehicle were desired prior to quantity production. The most important of these changes concerned the engine. In 1942, the US Army decided against an earlier ruling to use diesel engines in tanks instead of the usual petrol engines. It was feared that the supply of one type of fuel for tanks and another fuel for lorries would seriously complicate the logistical support of an armoured division. Although the United States produced many diesel-powered tanks during the Second World War almost all of these went to foreign armies under the Lend-Lease programme. By the 1950s, engine technology had reached the stage where large diesels were far more economical to run than comparably sized petrol engines. As a result, ATAC mated an M68 gun, an AVDS 1790-2 diesel and an M48 to result in the new XM60. The production model of this vehicle, the M60 Main Battle Tank, was more than just an up-armed and re-engined M48A2. It was a considerably improved vehicle with many small innovations and changes in manufacturing techniques. Probably the most evident changes were the new, flat rolled-plate glacis armour, the substitution of a larger M19 cupola for the old M1 cupola and a change in appearance of the wheels and mudguard line. Since the M60 was to replace both the M48 and the M103 in the new pentomic armoured division organization, the terms 'heavy tank' and 'medium tank' were dropped in favour of 'Main Battle Tank' or MBT. The M60 finally dispensed with the stereoscopic rangefinder, instead using a coincidence rangefinder. This type required more light, but was easier to use and was more effective in actual service.

The adoption of the 105mm gun lowered the amount of ammunition that could be carried in the M60. The turret was not as thickly armoured as the Army would have wished in the face of the new Soviet T-62 tank firing a hyper-velocity finned kinetic penetrator round, so a new turret with a pronounced rear bustle was accepted for production and entered service in 1962 as the M60A1. This type became the standard production model of the M60 family.

The only versions of the M60 to serve in Vietnam were the M728 engineer vehicle and the M60 AVLB bridgelayer.

Armour units in Germany received priority for the M60s. M48A3s were used by both Army and Marine tank units during the Vietnam War, when, terrain permitting, they were quite successful. There was no point in using the more powerful M60 since on the one occasion when American and North Vietnamese armour clashed, the M48 proved quite adequate. Numerous local improvizations were developed to add armour against mines or RPG-7 grenade launchers, but the only standardized change was the addition of a G350 turret cupola vision riser which gave the tank commander better 360° vision from within the cupola.

The T95 Project. In 1954, another new tank programme was initiated with an aim toward developing a tank lighter than the M48 but able to

fulfil the rôles of both the M48 and the M103. This new design was first called the TL-1, but subsequently became known as the T95. The vehicle was to be centred on several new smoothbore tank guns and a sophisticated OPTRAC light beam rangefinder. Its hull was low and sleek, reminiscent in many respects of the Soviet T-54. There were four basic versions built, including additional variations with experimental petrol and diesel engines and a hydro-pneumatic 'kneeling' suspension that allowed the tank to crouch and hide. The T95E1 used a smoothbore 90mm gun firing a hyper-velocity finned sub-calibre projectile. The original version placed the gun in a rigid mount without a conventional recoil system, but the recoil forces were found to severely damage the turret

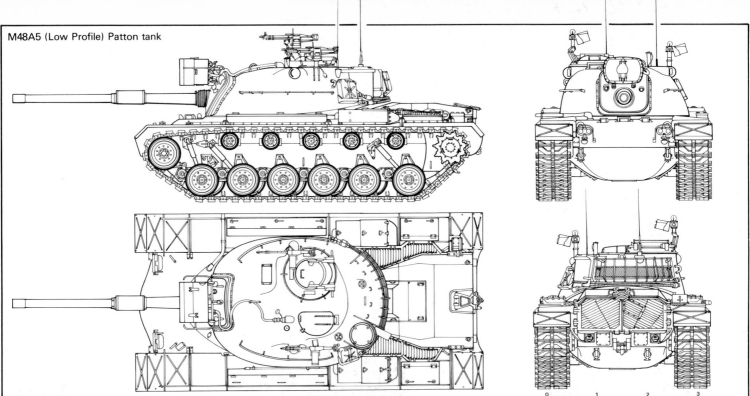

M48A5 (Low Profile) Patton tank

© STEVEN ZALOGA 1980

Left, top: The M48A5 programme re-manufactured earlier Pattons to make them suitable for tank combat in the 1980s. The most important change was the addition of an M68 105mm gun. The M48A5 is principally assigned to National Guard armoured units, not the Regular Army. These M48A5 (Low Profile) tanks of the 102nd Armor, 50th Armored Division (New Jersey National Guard) are taking part in exercises at Camp Drum, New York, in the summer of 1979. (Midic Castelletti)

Left, middle: Among the most successful variants of the M48 family has been the M88 armoured recovery vehicle. This particular machine is one of the new M88A1s, as is evident by the externally mounted smoke launchers on the bow. Eventually, these will be refitted to older types. (BMY)

Left, below: The T95 programme was an attempt to develop a smaller and lighter medium tank than the Patton series, incorporating many new fire control and gun technology advances. In many respects, the T95 was a direct counterpart of the Soviet T – 62. The initial version, as pictured here, was armed with a novel 90mm smoothbore gun. (R. J. Icks)

Right, top: Most of the T95 prototypes were armed with unconventional smoothbore cannon. Since this technology was unproven, one pilot vehicle, the T95E2, was fitted with the same turret as the M48A2 Patton to serve as a low-risk alternative to the other members of the series. (R. J. Icks)

Right, below: The M60 closely resembled the earlier Patton series, but was substantially redesigned in many respects. The most obvious points of difference are the larger M19 commander's cupola, the new mudguard line and redesigned road wheels. These M60s, supporting the 1st Infantry Division near Walkmuhle, Germany, during the 'Reforger V' manoeuvres in 1973, have been daubed with temporary mud camouflage. (US Army)

Left, top: The commander's enclosed cupola was not entirely popular with American tankers, and these M60s of the 2/33rd Armor, 3rd Armored Division during Operation 'Big Lift' in Germany, 1963, had improvized external pintle mounts for their .50 calibre machine-guns. The tank silhouette above the company tactical sign was an honorary designation, indicating qualification at the annual firing exercises at the Grafenwohr range. (US Army)

Left, below: The M60A1 was the backbone of the Israeli armoured force during the difficult fighting in 1973. This unit still has its tanks fitted with the M19 cupola, but it was removed in many units and replaced by an Israeli manufactured low profile cupola.(Israeli Defence Force)

Right: The M60A1 has been the principal main battle tank of US armoured divisions in Germany since the mid-1960s and will remain so until the mid-1980s, by which time it will be supplanted by the improved M60A3 and the new M1. This particular vehicle is one of the improved M60A1 (AOS) and has the thicker chin armour. It belongs to 4/69th Armor and is painted in the gaudy camouflage scheme that was peculiar to the Seventh Army in Germany in the late 1970s, prior to the introduction of the official new camouflage patterns. The regimental crest, a black panther on a green and white shield, is carried on the searchlight cover. (US Army)

Below: One vehicle in each M60 tank company is provided with a bulldozer blade to help entrench the unit's tanks. This particular M60A1 is taking firing practice at the Yakima ranges in Washington, 1977. Note that the infra-red VSS − 2 searchlight has been removed and stowed at the rear of the turret. (US Army)

Above: In the 1970s, the Marines finally received M60A1s to replace their ageing M48s and M103A2s. These M60A1s of the 2nd Marine Tank Battalion are on summer exercises in Norway in 1976. (USMC)

Left: One of the specialized variants of the M60 series is the M728 combat engineer vehicle. It closely resembles the M60A1 but is fitted with an A-frame jib boom and a 165mm howitzer. Here, an M728 at the Engineer Training Grounds, Fort Belvoir, Virginia, removes a wrecked M151 jeep. (US Army)

Right, top: With troubles brewing in the Middle East, the Marines have been undergoing more extensive desert training. Here a pair of M48A3s of the 4th Tank Battalion, 4th Marine Division, take part in the Operation 'Palm Tree III' manoeuvres in California during 1976; note that they are wearing the new tank camouflage paint. (USMC)

Right: M48A5s of the 50th Armored Division take target practice at Fort Drum in 1977. One point of interest is that the spent shell casings are of the new aluminium type instead of the traditional (and expensive) brass. (US Army)

The MBT – 70 Project. In 1963, after several failed attempts to replace the long-lived M26 – M46 – M47 – M48 – M60 series with a wholly new design, the Army tried again. This time the effort was jointly conducted with the Bundeswehr, with the West German government contributing about thirty per cent of the research and development costs. The new tank, called MBT – 70 or Kampfpanzer 70, was initiated during the McNamara era at the Pentagon. The buzz words in those days were 'technological imperative' and the new MBT – 70 was going to be chock-a-block with every nifty little gadget the designers could dream up. The Air Force could have its supersonic fighters, and the Navy its carriers, so the Army wanted its own prestige weapon as well. The MBT – 70 programme differed from most previous Army tank efforts in that it incorporated a greater number of new, unproven technologies. The earlier T95 programme had been far more modest in comparison. The MBT – 70 was to have full weapon stabilization to allow for fire-on-the-move. It was to incorporate an automatic loader, be totally protected in a contaminated environment, have a 'kneeling' hydro-pneumatic suspension and layered armour. Its main gun was to be the ill-fated Shillelagh gun/missile launcher, which would entangle other Army tank efforts in a nightmare of technical problems. The grim tale of the Shillelagh is told more fully here in the section dealing with the M551 (page 32). While all the features planned for the MBT – 70 were very desirable from a technical and tactical standpoint, there was inadequate

consideration of whether these costly features would add significantly to the combat effectiveness of the vehicle as a whole in order to justify their use. Management of the programme was further hurt by the usual problems which crop-up in joint-development programmes. Many of the technical solutions adopted to solve tactical problems were too extreme. For example, the tank was supposed to be protected by an NBC filtration system; someone came up with the novel idea of placing the driver up in the turret with the rest of the crew, creating only a single compartment to protect against airborne contaminants. This simplified the NBC protection system, but in so doing created a hellish engineering problem with the driving controls and clutch. The driver's station in the turret had to be stabilized so that it remained pointing forward, and the controls had to be articulated to follow the turret around! The vehicle was to be powered by a new multi-fuel engine, but the partners could not agree on who would manufacture the engine. The German automatic loader failed to function properly, and technical problems in one system inevitably manifested themselves elsewhere in the design. The trials in 1968 moved forward in fits and starts as each new technical stumbling-block was overcome. But by 1969, the programme costs had escalated to five times those initially agreed upon, and the Germans withdrew. The Bundeswehr was beginning to receive its new Leopard MBTs and felt no particular pressure to field another new tank. The US Congress urged the Army to terminate the

programme, especially since the mounting costs of the Vietnam War were cutting into more fruitful ventures. The Army agreed to develop a more austere version, called the XM803, which dispensed with such gimmicks as the retractable remote control 20mm autocannon at the rear of the turret. Chrysler offered an even more austere 'K Tank', and in 1971 Congress finally cut funding. Had the MBT – 70 programme been the only trouble-spot in the Army tank programme, it might have endured a little longer, but it occurred at a time when Congress was looking for scalps over the fiasco with the M60A2 missile tank and M551 Sheridan problems. If production plans had proceeded, the MBT – 70 would have cost more than three times as much as the M60, and in constant-dollar terms would have been considerably more expensive than today's M1 Abrams tank. It wound up after over a quarter of a billion dollars had been spent, and led to far more critical Congressional oversight of the Army's tank effort.

The M60A2 and M60A3 Main Battle Tanks. While problems over the Shillelagh missile/gun system were only a contributory factor in the demise of the MBT – 70, they had a crippling effect on the M60 programme. In 1964 the Army decided that the Shillelagh system, which had originally been designed for the M551 AR/AAV, would offer better long-range accuracy than the gun currently used on the M60A1. The programme to re-gun the M60 was called XM66 and several versions were developed. Proposals A and B used a new 'compact' turret with

Left, top: This M60A1 of Company B, 5/1st Cavalry, is taking part in training manoeuvres at Fort Hood, Texas, in August 1975 and sports a dust-encrusted coat of the new MERDC four-tone camouflage pattern. (US Army)

Left, below: A weary and ragged looking XM1 takes part in firing demonstrations during its trials in 1979. This pilot vehicle incorporates some of the new design changes, such as the filter improvements and the new drive sprocket, that were added to correct flaws uncovered during the tests.

Above: The MBT – 70 was one of the most sophisticated tanks ever designed. The driver's stabilized compartment in the turret and the remote control 20mm cannon position behind it were among the extravagant features that added unnecessary cost and complexity to the design, and led to its demise. (US Army)

Right: Several turret configurations were examined during the XM66 development programme, including this conventional turret mounted on an M48A3 hull. (Bob McDonald)

improved ballistic shape, better armour protection and lighter weight than the M60A1 turret; Proposal C was for a more conventionally shaped turret, but had a slaved 20mm autocannon at the turret rear, as on the two earlier proposals; and Proposal D was a modified M60A1 turret armed with the Shillelagh system. The Army opted for Proposal A, feeling that the reduced turret weight would add measurably to the vehicle's mobility. The Shillelagh system firing a guided anti-tank missile had a better than eighty per cent probability of a hit on a target at 1,500m, while the 105mm gun on the M60A1 firing an APDS round had about a seventy-five per cent hit probability. What impressed the Army more was that the M60A1's accuracy beyond this range dropped off precipitously, while the XM66's missile retained a good deal of accuracy as far as 3,000m. The programme was believed to be a 'low-risk venture', merely concerned with repackaging existing hardware. A premature production authorization led to 300 hulls and 243 turrets being manufactured before the vehicle had been adequately tested. The plan was to re-equip a number of older M60s with the new turret, and transfer the M60 turrets with their 105mm gun over to some old M48s, to result in M48A4s. This plan tied up the older hulls as well as the new vehicles. The problems stemmed from complications in the development of conventional non-missile rounds for the gun. The conventional rounds jarred the turret and upset the fire controls, and their consumable casings frequently coated the interior of the tube with hot débris that prematurely 'cooked off' other rounds. A scavenger system was added to the breech to circumvent this problem, and air compressor equipment fitted in a bustle at the rear of the engine compartment. The delay in solving the problems led to the decision to drop the M48A4 scheme after a few prototypes had been built, but the XM66 programme itself continued, finally resulting in the M60A2. Although production had begun in 1966, the first M60A2 did not enter service until eight years later in 1974. There were 540 M60A2s built, and the majority were used to form six-tank battalions stationed in Germany. The

complexity of the M60A2 led to the nickname 'Starship'. Rather than supplant the M60A1, the M60A2 programme only served to slow down production of much needed main battle tanks. The vehicle continues to be plagued by problems, particularly in regards to the recoil system. Technical improvements in the fire controls on the M60A1 and new ammunition technology have lessened the advantage the M60A2 enjoys in long-range duels. Ironically, in 1980, the US Army considered rebuilding the M60A2s with M48 turrets and 105mm guns.

The troubled trio of the M551, MBT – 70 and M60A2 had profound and unfortunate effects on the Army's tank effort. The Vietnam War drained funds away from tank procurement for the armoured divisions configured for European missions, and expectancy over the MBT – 70 and M60A2 slowed production of the M60A1. These failings were camouflaged by low inventory goals. At the same time, the Soviet Army was undergoing a major conventional arms modernization effort after the change in orientation from Khruschev's nuclear arms bias. The Soviets began fielding the new T – 62 in large numbers, further enlarging the numerical gap between the tank forces of the US and USSR, while narrowing the qualitative gap that the United States had once enjoyed. The supply to Israel of replacement M60A1s after the heavy losses in the 1973 war further exacerbated the problem. In the light of the cost and dubious success of the M60A2 project, and the expensive débâcle with MBT – 70, Congress was in a very unsympathetic mood when Army representatives approached for more tank funds to acquire the decade-old M60A1 as well as research funds for a new main battle tank effort. However, Congress could do little but agree in view of the Soviet 4-to-1 advantage in tanks.

Once again, the hefty size of the M48/M60 series lent itself nicely to further evolutionary growth. The large size of American tanks compared to their European counterparts is due to two main reasons. In the 1940s, when the M26/M46 family was first developed, the US Army favoured bulkier air-cooled engines, while most European designers preferred

smaller liquid-cooled power plants. Secondly, American tanks have traditionally been designed to accommodate the '95 percentile man'. In other words, ninety-five per cent of US soldiers could serve as crews in the tanks; a 95 percentile man is defined as 6ft 1in and 200lb. In contrast, most Soviet tanks are designed around a 25 – 30 percentile man: 5ft 7in, and weighing 150lb. The new modernization effort was to encompass the M48 as well, bringing them up to M60 standards for the armoured divisions of the National Guard. The basic conversion, of course, was the addition of the M68 105mm gun, though in the case of older M48A1s a new engine and other internal improvements were necessary. The new version was to be called the M48A5. The conversion of M48A3s to A5s consisted of the new gun and mount, a reticle sight, an electrical kit, a new turret basket, new ammunition stowage, a gun travel lock, a solid-state engine regulator, and new T142 replaceable pad track. Externally, the M48A5 can be distinguished from the older M48A3 by its new gun, the gun travel lock on the rear deck and the top loading air filters. During the course of re-manufacturing, the Army decided to adopt a low profile tank commander's cupola, similar to that used on the original M48, as the result of experiences of Israeli tankers who roundly criticized the M1 cupola. The initial batch of M48A5 (serials A3001 to A3999) were still fitted with the M1 cupola and G350 turret riser, and had the older model AVDS 1790 – 2A engine. The later batch, called M48A5 (Low Profile), had the new, flat cupola, two M60D pintle mounted machine-guns and the later 1790 – 2D diesel. By 1979, 1,573 M48A5s had been manufactured for the National Guard, as well as several hundred others for foreign clients. Similar modification efforts have been undertaken by other M48 Patton users, notably the German M48A2G2 programme and the Israeli modification programme begun in 1967.

The modification programme on the M60A1 was gradual and began in 1971. The first improvement was the addition of a top-loading air filter in 1971, followed by an Add-On Stabilization (or AOS) system. There had been repeated attempts to

develop a gun stabilization system on American tanks since the ill-fated gyro stabilizers tried on the Sherman in 1942. The AOS system on the M60A1 allows the tank to fire accurately while on the move. This is an important virtue in tank combat, since a moving vehicle is a far less vulnerable target than a stationary one. The final improvement in this phase, the T142 replaceable pad track, was added in 1974, resulting in the M60A1 (AOS). The next phase was the addition of a 'reliability improvement of selected equipment' (RISE) engine, the AVDS 1790–2D with an improved electrical harness. This resulted in the M60A1 (RISE). Finally, in 1977, the vehicle was equipped with passive night sights and a deep water-fording kit, resulting in the final configuration of the M60A1 series, the M60A1 (RISE Passive). The new night fighting equipment consisted of an M35E1 gunner/TC night sight and AN/VVS–2 driver's sight. Both these systems are image intensification sights and function by amplifying ambient starlight. Unlike previous infra-red systems, they require no illumination from the tank which would allow their detection by enemy anti-tank gunners. The M60A1 still remains equipped with an AN/VSS–2A infra-red searchlight and infra-red viewers to serve as a back-up in case the new passive sets fail or if there is not enough starlight for the passive viewers to function. The product improved M60A1s have also been up-armoured, but details of this are still classified. During the 1973 Arab-Israeli War, the M60A1 was found to be well armoured except in the chin area under the front of the turret and the turret ring, which suffered a disproportionate number of penetrations. An additional armour fillet is being added under the chin to correct this, and the turret ring casting is being thickened. Since 1979, the product improved M60A1s have been receiving M239 smoke launchers, which are an American derivative of the type used on the British Chieftain tank.

In 1978, the next stage of M60A1 modification led to a re-classification of the vehicle from M60A1 to M60A3. This stage involved the addition of a ruby laser rangefinder, a solid-state ballistic computer, a thermal sleeve for the gun barrel to prevent heat warpage, and a new M240 coaxial machine-gun. The laser rangefinder replaced the coincidence rangefinder, and is fired from the right-hand side sighting blister. In 1979, another new configuration reached the assembly line, the M60A3 (TTS or Tank Thermal Sight). On this version, the M35E1 passive night sight was replaced by AN/VSG–2 (TTS), and the tank had an engine smoke generator added, similar to those on Soviet tanks. The TTS sight is a passive night sight that forms an amplified, coherent image for the gunner and tank commander by sensing incident infra-red emissions from the area being viewed. All natural and man-made objects give off a certain amount of infra-red energy (heat), and the TTS works by distinguishing between the levels of infra-red energy being emitted. Such a sight is particularly useful in tank combat, since it does not rely on ambient light levels and can be used on pitch-black nights. Tanks and vehicles give off very distinctive infra-red signatures, and the sight can be used in daylight to sense through smoke, fog or light mist. The M60A3 was the first production tank to be fitted with such a sight. The M60A3 had other fire control improvements added, including a meteorological sensor that automatically feeds the computer such data as wind drift for gun adjustments when firing.

The M60A3 has the same internal arrangement as the M48 and other variants of the M60 family. The driver sits in the front centre of the hull, with the turret fighting compartment behind him and the engine compartment at the rear containing the engine and transmission. In front of the driver is the glacis armour plate with an equivalent armour thickness of 230mm. On either side are protected ammunition stowage tubes for the main gun. The M60A3 is more heavily armoured than the T–62, which has an equivalent glacis armour thickness of 200mm. The driver steers the tank by means of a simple wheel control. The controls are power-assisted and the tank uses an automatic transmission. This consumes more fuel than the

Left: The M60A2 programme was among the most troubled of the entire M60 family. Unanticipated problems with the revolutionary gun/missile armament system severely delayed the programme and reduced its scope. One of the more successful aspects of the programme was the well designed and thickly armoured configuration of the new turret. (Chrysler Corporation)
Top: Among the prominent features of the M60A2 were the commander's large cupola and the short, stubby gun tube. The small container above the gun tube houses the transmitter used to track and guide the Shillelagh missile round. The flags flown from this vehicle were used during firing training. (Brian Gibbs)
Middle: Although the main change incorporated on the M60A2 was the new turret, the rear engine area was modified by the addition of compressor equipment to work the bore scavanger system, which applied air pressure to eject any remaining bits of débris from the barrel of the gun. This particular vehicle served with 1/67th Armor, 2nd Armored Division, at Fort Hood, Texas, in 1975. (Brian Gibbs)
Bottom: The principal changes on the new M60A3 are mainly internal and are related to the fire control system. Nevertheless, there are several external changes evident, such as the small port for the laser rangefinder in place of the old rangefinder port, the thermal sleeve for the gun, the new smoke dischargers and the top-loading air filters. The M60A3 also uses the newer VSS–3A infra-red searchlight. Some of these features, such as the filters and smoke dischargers, are being retrofitted to the older M60A1. (George Woodard)

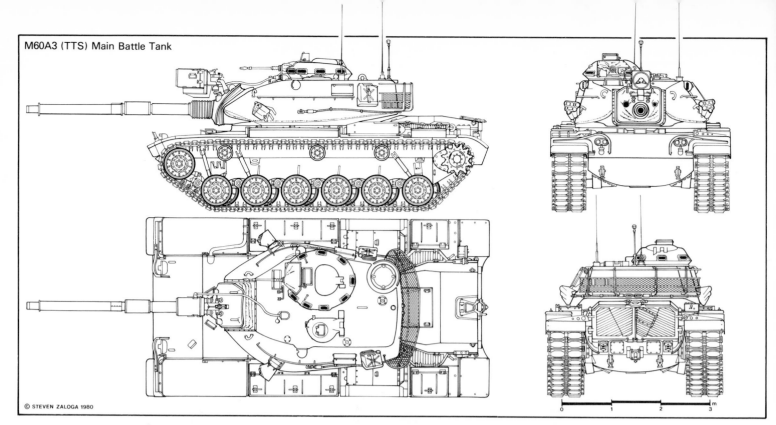

M60A3 (TTS) Main Battle Tank

© STEVEN ZALOGA 1980

0   1   2   3
m

Left, top: The M60A3 (TTS) is the most advanced version of the M60 family now in service, though further modernization efforts are likely to continue through the 1980s. Since the adoption of the MERDC four-colour camouflage patterns, the paint colour for uncamouflaged equipment has changed from the traditional Olive Drab to Forest Green. (ATAC-PM-M-60 Office)

Right: An M60A1 of the 2nd Platoon, C Company, 4/73rd Armor, during summer exercises near Grafenwohr, Germany, 1976. The barrel stripes indicate the platoon, while the vehicle name ('Crustacean') signifies the company. The cartoon on the turret side is a Second World War rhomboid tank pictured as a snail, and was the work of the vehicle's gunner, Brian Gibbs. (Brian Gibbs)

Left, below: An M60A1 of the 1st Platoon, C Company, 4/73rd Armor, fitted with the mounting attachment for a bulldozer blade. The blade was generally left off except when specifically required, since, in the event of hydraulic failure, the blade would drop, giving the crew a nasty surprise. This vehicle is finished in the temporary four-tone colour scheme peculiar to the Seventh Army in Germany. The two tank silhouettes with wreathes indicate qualification with distinction at two consecutive years' gunnery trials. (Brian Gibbs)

rudimentary clutch and brake system used on the Soviet T−62, but is much simpler to operate, prevents rapid driver fatigue and is simpler for the crew to maintain. The manual transmission used on the T−62 is the most frequent source of mechanical breakdowns on Soviet tanks. The steering system is difficult to operate and the driver's compartment is small, poorly ventilated and not well suited to prolonged combat driving. The M60A3 driver has three sets of vision devices: a daylight periscope, an infra-red converter for use when the infra-red lights are on, and a passive night viewer. The turret on the M60A3 is provided with a full basket. The gunner is stationed in the front right-hand side of the turret, with the tank commander immediately behind him and slightly above. The gun-loader is stationed in the left half of the turret with a ready rack of ammunition at his feet along the edge of the turret basket, and additional ammunition stowage in a bin on the floor in front of him and in racks in the turret bustle. In comparison with the T−62, the gun loader's station in the M60A3 is much better laid out for a higher rate of fire and for prolonged gun usage. The American gunner rams home the round with his right arm, while his Soviet counterpart, who is stationed in the opposite side of the turret, must use his left. As mentioned earlier, American tanks are configured for larger crewmen, which is an important feature to be kept in mind when it is realized that modern tank ammunition weighs about 25kg per round.

The rôle of the tank commander is to observe and direct the actions of the crew. He is provided with 360° view by use of vision devices in the M19 cupola. The cupola is fitted with a .50 calibre machine-gun for use against troops, lightly armoured vehicles or low-flying aircraft and helicopters. Some thought was given to replacing the M19 cupola with a low-profile cupola, but this idea was dropped. The commander is provided with a set of dual controls, which allow him to aim and fire the main gun should this prove necessary. The usual procedure in an engagement is otherwise. The commander acquires a target, and swings the turret in the correct direction by hydraulic control, while telling the loader which type of ammunition to chamber. The ammunition type is fed into the ballistic computer by either the commander or gunner; the computer stores the ballistic performance data on four basic types of ammunition plus six related types. The only factors that are manually indexed into the computer are air temperature and air pressure, but as these do not vary greatly from moment to moment, they can be indexed into the computer in advance. The gunner acquires the target in his sight, which is bore-sighted to the commander's laser sight. Either the commander or gunner triggers the laser. The range

is fed into the computer automatically, unless there are multiple readings due to obstructions such as trees, in which case the commander selects the proper reading and manually feeds it into the computer. While these procedures are taking place, the computer is determining gun correction through the use of automatic sensors. The gun stabilization system, keyed to an inertial gyro platform, keeps the gun stationary in relation to vehicle movement. If the tank is stationary but the target moving, a rate unit computes lead angles as the gunner manually follows the target. The crosswind sensor on the turret roof provides inputs regarding wind velocity that will affect the flight of the projectile, and the cant unit senses gun trunnion roll should the tank be resting unevenly to one side. The computer then projects a reticle onto the gunner's sight, which takes into account all factors affecting the firing of the round. The gunner then uses his controls to put the reticle on the target, and fires the gun. The entire firing sequence takes about fifteen seconds. The probability of a first-round kill against a T−62 at 1,500m firing an APDS round such as the M735 is about seventy-five per cent, compared to a forty-six per cent probability of a T−62 scoring a first-round kill against an M60A1 under the same conditions. The probability of an M60A2 firing a Shillelagh guided missile round is comparable to the performance of the M60A3. At 3,000m, the M60A3 has about a fifty per cent first-round hit probability against a T−62, while for a T−62 its probability is less than ten per cent. The T−62 uses a rudimentary stadiametric system based on a ballistic reticle not much different from that used on the Sherman tank in 1942. Only recently have T−62s been fitted with ballistic computers of the simple analogue type used on the early M48, and only in the past few years have some T−62s been fitted with a laser rangefinder in place of the ballistic reticle ranging system.

In terms of armour protection, the M60A3 is a larger target, but it is as mobile as the T−62 and more thickly armoured. The M60A3 also has greater barrel depression, so that in hull defilade it presents a much smaller target. In terms of equivalent effective armour thickness, the M60A3 has 230mm on the hull front versus 200mm for the T−62, in excess of 260mm on the turret front versus 230mm on the T−62, and 140mm versus 120mm on the turret sides. Since all of the M60A3's fuel is stowed internally, it does not have the fuel hazard posed by the T−62's externally stowed fuel tanks. American tanks have a decided advantage in overall reliability, with the M60A3 enjoying an MTBF (Mean Time Between Failures) of about 960km. It is estimated that the T−62's MTBF ranges from between a half to a quarter of this. Combat experience against the T−62 in 1973 left the Israeli tank force quite

confident of the M60A1, though there were problems, subsequently corrected, with the hydraulic system. American tanks use a high-pressure hydraulic system to traverse the turret which, it is felt, provides much quicker acquisition of targets. However, in 1973 it was found that when the system was ruptured by battle damage, a fine mist of volatile fluid was sprayed into the turret which was readily ignited, severely burning the crew. A new fluid with a higher flashpoint was developed after the war.

A comparison between the M60A3 and the newer Soviet T−64 and T−72 is more difficult to make owing to the lack of precise information on these designs. American tank officers testifying before Congress have indicated that they feel the M60A3 is a superior tank in most respects, with the possible exception of armour. It is likely that the new Soviet tanks enjoy higher road speeds than the M60A3, but in view of past Soviet design failings it would not be surprising if they have the same transmission and suspension shortcomings of earlier types and currently suffer the consequent teething pains. The overall accuracy of the 125mm gun on these tanks is likely to be an improvement over the T−62, due to the addition of a laser rangefinder and ballistic computer, but evidence regarding the use of a stabilization system to provide fire-on-the-move capability is not yet conclusive. The T−64 and T−72 both feature an automatic loader, but US Intelligence officials indicate that there has been evidence of problems with this feature seriously jeopardizing crew safety. The big question is whether or not the vehicles are fitted with an early generation of composite armour using layers of steel and ceramic. Some feel that if they are armoured in this fashion, they could pose a serious threat to NATO anti-tank weapons, which use shaped-charge warheads. American tankers are less worried, as the M60 relies on kinetic energy rounds for anti-tank fighting, and are confident that the new generation of ammunition can handle this type of armour. Intelligence analysts feel that the T−64 and T−72 mark a break in Soviet design philosophy, from sacrificing higher quality for numerical superiority to favouring more sophisticated and costly designs at the expense of lower annual Soviet tank production.

While many of the advantages of the M60A3 over the earlier M60A1 have come in the area of fire control, there have been important strides in ammunition technology that have improved the capabilities of the M60A1 and M48A5 as well. The main anti-tank round used by the US Army is the M735A1, which is a hyper-velocity discarding-sabot armour-piercing round using a depleted uranium core. Depleted uranium (DU) is frequently given the euphemistic name 'staballoy' in the United States after ill-informed press commentary linked it to atomic weapons. Depleted uranium is used instead of the usual tungsten carbide because it is a tougher, denser material. Another advantage is that it has pyrophoric qualities. The friction on penetration of the target is so high that it ignites the metal, spraying the inside of the tank with small shards of burning metal. The M735A1 round will eventually be superceded by the M774 round, which is composed entirely of depleted uranium. The United States is also working on an even more advanced kinetic penetrator round, the XM883, which is expected to offer a major leap forward in penetration and accuracy at long range. The advances in fire control and ammunition technology have achieved a degree of accuracy and lethality that was earlier secured at much greater cost and complexity with the M60A2's Shillelagh missile.

The US Army plans to modify about 1,980 M60A1s to M60A3 standards and to manufacture a total of about 1,700 new M60A3s, for a total of about 3,700 M60A3s by 1985. M60A3s have already been promised to Egypt, Israel, Saudi Arabia and Jordan. This will give the United States a tank force consisting of about 3,700 M60A3s, 4,000 M60A1 (RISE Passive), 1,554 M60s, 540 M60A2s and 1,600 M48A5s in the mid 1980s. Production of the new M1 Abrams was begun in 1980 and will add to this total. The Army does not currently plan to bring up to A3 standards all of its M60A1s, since the modifications are costly, and they would prefer to see the money spent on buying more M1 Abrams tanks. Nevertheless, M60s will make up nearly sixty per cent of the US Army inventory until the 1990s, so it is likely that further product improvement programmes will eventually take place. Among the possibilities already developed are a muzzle reference system, which would increase accuracy by about 10 – 20 per cent, a land navigation system and an NBC protection system. ATAC developed plans for an M60 with a composite armour turret, similar to that fitted to the M1, called the M60AN. There have also been automotive redesigns studied, including an Improved Mobility M60A1 incorporating a hydro-pneumatic suspension and 1,200 horsepower diesel engine that would raise the M60's maximum cross-country speed to an impressive 40km/hr. The Army is also developing an M60 armed with the 120mm gun, which is being fitted in the M1E1. The M60 family is likely to be in service in one form or another well into the 1990s.

The M1 Abrams. In December 1971, three months after Congress killed the XM803 effort, the Army was authorized to begin the design of a new main battle tank. This effort was initially called the MGT – 75 (Medium Gun Tank 75) and aimed at developing a new tank for about half a million dollars each in 1972 dollars. In response to the MBT – 70 fiasco, Congress impressed upon the Army the need to keep the vehicle relatively simple and to bring it into production in as short a time as possible. The Army answered by formulating a 'concurrent' design and test programme in which the engineering and operational tests would run simultaneously rather than sequentially, thereby saving about three years. An Army task force drew up a set of design criteria for the new vehicle, and in June 1973 Chrysler and General Motors were awarded contracts for the construction of prototype vehicles that would be competitively tested before the final engineering development contract was awarded. While this competitive development technique was often used on other weapon systems, it was fairly novel in the tank business. By this time the tank had become known as the XM1. The GM prototype was powered by a conventional diesel engine, while the Chrysler prototypes used a unique turbine power plant.

The 1973 Arab-Israeli War had resulted in a great deal of uninformed press speculation about the demise of the tank in the face of cheap guided anti-tank missiles such as the Soviet 9M14M Malyutka (AT – 4 Sagger). Since 1947, ATAC had been developing composite armours using layers of metallic and non-metallic armour plate to defeat the type of shaped-charge warheads used in anti-tank missiles. These had been experimentally tested on the T95. In the early 1970s, British engineers made a

Top: The M60AX is a private venture by Teledyne Continental to upgrade the M60 with additional armour to resist the 125mm round of the new Soviet T – 64 and T – 72. It incorporates numerous automotive improvements, such as a new engine, new suspension and other features. Besides offering improved ballistic protection, the package enhances the vehicle's cross-country mobility.
Middle: The General Motors entry in the XM1 competition was a highly successful design but, in the end, it lost to the turbine-powered Chrysler version. (Detroit Diesel Allison)
Bottom: The development problems of the MBT – 70 led Congress to keep an especially close eye on the XM1 trials. Here, prototype number 9 goes through its paces in the mud at Fort Knox. (George Woodard)
Right, top: The initial pilot vehicle of the XM1 rests outside the Detroit Army Test Plant prior to trials in 1978. The US Army's requirement for high vehicle reliability led to the XM1 pilot vehicles being subjected to the most strenuous tests ever conducted on a new tank design. (US Army)
Right, middle: With the advent of heat-seeking anti-tank missiles near at hand, the M1 Abrams features conscious design characteristics, such as the use of less conspicuous exhaust outlets at the rear, to minimize its infra-red signature. While engine problems caused some anxiety over the fate of the XM1, by the time of the 1979 trials these troubles had been largely resolved. (George Woodard)
Right, bottom: Compared to Soviet tanks, American tanks are spacious inside, since this enhances crew efficiency under prolonged combat conditions and reduces safety problems. This interior view of the turret of an M1 Abrams is taken from the loader's position, and shows the gunner at his station peering into his telescopic sight. Resting on the commander's seat is a CVC helmet (DH 132). Beside the gunner is the ballistic computer and thermal sight (on the right), and the breech of the M68A1 105mm gun (on the left). The commander's controls and sighting equipment are evident behind him. (Office of the Secretary of Defense)

major breakthrough in this technology, resulting in the so-called Chobham armour. On the basis of British research, American engineers developed an improved composite armour that was adopted on both the General Motors and Chrysler prototypes. In 1975, the US held a series of tests to determine which tank gun would be adopted on the XM1. The tests included several new British guns, the German L11 Rheinmetall gun being adopted on the Leopard II, and the M68 gun used on the M60A1. The surprise results of these tests were those achieved by the old M68 gun when firing the new M735 and M744 rounds. The Army decided to retain the M68 on the XM1, but stipulated that the turrets would have to be designed to accommodate the German 120mm gun at a later date. The Americans preferred the German gun over its British competitors, not so much due to any technical superiority but because it was further along in its developmental cycle and standardization with the Bundeswehr made more sense as it fields over three times as many tanks as the British Army. In 1974, the American and German governments agreed to attempt to standardize as many components as possible between their new tank designs, and the Germans were permitted to enter a modified version of their Leopard II into the XM1 competition.

In February 1976, the first XM1 prototype vehicles were turned over to the Army for competitive trials which began immediately. The German entry, the Leopard II AV (American Version), did not arrive until September 1976. The Army was sceptical of the prospects of the Leopard II AV, since it had not been designed around the criteria laid down for the American entries; for example, it lacked full ammunition compartmentalization. The Germans did not feel that their entry was judged fairly, and the arguments and recriminations over the matter did not help the standardization issue. There was controversy within the Pentagon over which of the American entries to choose, as both had performed well in the tests. The Army, after the sobering experience of the MBT–70 failure, preferred the General Motors design because its diesel engine was viewed as a lower developmental risk. The civilian officials within the Department of Defence favoured the Chrysler vehicle, feeling that even though its turbine engine was not as mature, in the long run there would be technical and tactical advantages in adopting a turbine. Turbine engines are much quieter than diesels, are about a ton lighter in this power range, are expected to last two-and-a-half times longer without an overhaul compared to diesels, have transmission advantages and are easier to repair and maintain. On the debit side, they consume more fuel but their smaller engine size allows more fuel to be carried. The Department of Defense had its way and, in November 1976, the contract for full-scale engineering development went to Chrysler.

The engineering and operational tests were run concurrently in 1978 and 1979 and, as the Army had feared, there were problems with the turbine engine. The principal problem was not with the engine itself, but rather with the interface between the filters and the engine, which leaked in dust and débris, damaging the turbine blades. Army officials were run over the coals in front of Congress, which was especially sensitive to any hints of trouble after the misfortunes of the Army's tank effort in the 1960s. Much of the criticism of the programme was overblown, in view of the early stage of the vehicle's development, and the fact that the XM1 underwent more strenuous testing than virtually any other tank design. The problems were somewhat exaggerated by the concurrent engineering and operational testing; in a less hurried situation, many of the technical problems would have been cured in the engineering testing, and would not have repeated themselves in the operational phase, as happened with the XM1. By the end of 1979, the XM1's problems with the engine and tracks had largely been resolved, and Congress gave the go-ahead for initial production. The first M1 Abrams tank came off the assembly lines in February 1980. The M1 was named after General Creighton Abrams, who had commanded the 37th Tank Battalion, 4th Armored

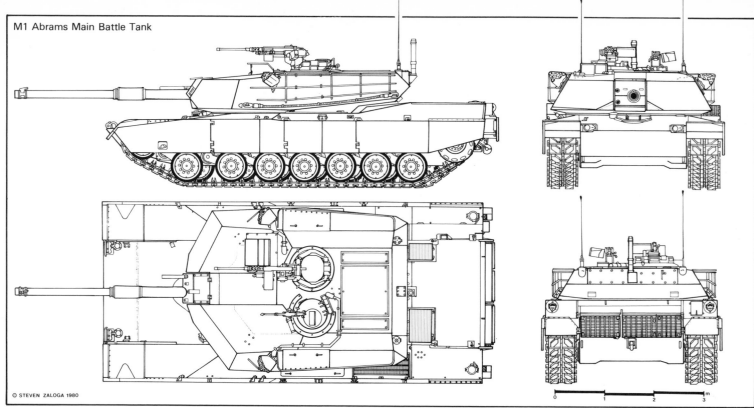

M1 Abrams Main Battle Tank

© STEVEN ZALOGA 1980

0   1   2   3 m

Above: Pilot vehicle number 7 moves down a dirt road at over 70km/hr. The M1 is among the fastest tanks in the world today due to its potent 1,500 horsepower turbine engine, and, surprisingly, one of the quietest. (ATAC-PM-XM1 Office)

Left: Pilot vehicle 9 is shown here in the four-tone camouflage scheme adopted by the US Army in the late 1970s. Several design changes were incorporated into the production M1s as a result of the XM1 trials in 1978 and 1979. (ATAC-PM-XM1 Office)

Below: 1. 25mm Armour-Piercing Fin Stabilized Discarding Sabot round used on the M2 and M3 25mm automatic cannon. It is believed to be capable of penetrating 75mm of steel armour at 0° obliquity at 1,000m.

2. The kinetic penetrator – composed of depleted uranium – for the 25mm round.

3. M319 76mm Armour Piercing Discarding Sabot round used by the M41 tank. It weighs 8.7kg, with an initial muzzle velocity of 1,257m/sec and a penetration of 70mm of steel armour at 0° at 1,000m.

4. A cross-sectional view of a 76mm telescoped round developed for the automatic cannon on the HSTV-L light tank test bed.

5. M332A1 90mm Armour-Piercing Discarding Sabot-Tracer round used by the M48 tank. It weighs 14.65kg with an initial muzzle velocity of 1,165m/sec and is believed capable of penetrating 160mm of steel armour at 0° obliquity at 1,000m.

6. M348 90mm High Explosive Anti-Tank round used by the M48 tank. Weighing 15.8kg, it has a shaped-charge warhead of .7kg of Comp 'B' explosive. The initial muzzle velocity is 832m/sec with a penetration of about 190mm of steel at 0° obliquity at 1,000m.

7. M735A1 105mm Armour-Piercing Discarding Sabot Fin Stabilized round used by the M60A1 and M48A5 tanks. It weighs approximately 24kg, with an approximate initial muzzle velocity of about 1,500m/sec and penetration of steel of perhaps 370mm at 0° at 1,000m. The M774 round is essentially similar in appearance but is composed entirely of depleted uranium, while the M735A1 uses only a depleted uranium core. The older M735 used a tungsten carbide core.

8. The kinetic penetrator portion of the 105mm M735A1 round.

9. M456A1 105mm High Explosive Anti-Tank round used on the M60A1 tank. It weighs 21.8kg, has a shaped-charge warhead containing .97kg of Comp 'B' explosive with an initial muzzle velocity of 1,173m/sec and an armour penetration against steel of perhaps 430mm at 0° obliquity at 1,000m.

10. The 152mm Shillelagh MGM – 51A guided anti-tank round with fins folded, as used in the M60A2 and M551 tanks. It weighs 26.8kg, has an initial muzzle velocity of 689m/sec with steel armour penetration estimated at about 430mm at 0° obliquity.

11. M409 152mm High Explosive Anti-Tank Tracer Multi-Purpose round used by the M60A2 and M551 tanks. It weighs 22kg, has a shaped-charge round containing 2.85kg of Comp 'B' explosive with an initial muzzle velocity of 683m/sec and a steel armour penetration estimated at about 430mm at 0° obliquity.

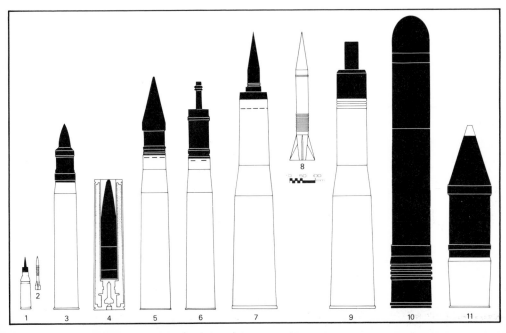

Division, during the famous drive to relieve Bastogne during the Battle of the Bulge in 1944, but who is better remembered as the commander of US troops in Vietnam.

In respect to firepower, the M1 is fairly comparable to the M60A3 (TTS), although its fire control system is better integrated into the design and employs a full-solution ballistic computer and other improvements. For example, a muzzle reference system used in place of a thermal sleeve which senses barrel droop caused by heat warpage. This adds about 10 – 20 per cent to the accuracy of the system. The stabilization system is designed to operate at much higher speeds. The main advances in the M1 over the M60A3 are in respect to mobility and armoured protection. The M1 is officially acknowledged to have a maximum road speed of 73km/hr, but is known to be capable of speeds in excess of 90km/hr. It is capable of cross-country speeds of over 50km/hr, and employs an improved torsion bar suspension which has double the road wheel travel of the M60, giving a much smoother ride. In comparison, the M60A3 has a maximum road speed of 50km/hr, and a cross-country speed of 15km/hr.

The entire frontal arc of the M1 is protected by composite armour. This subject is still tightly classified, but from published sources it would appear to consist of spaced layers of conventional rolled homogeneous steel armour layered with plates of ceramic armour that deflect the super-heated gas blasts of shaped-charge warheads. To test this armour, the Army placed an M1 on a firing-range and shelled it with a complete range of Soviet tank guns and anti-tank missiles. There were no penetrations in the frontal attacks even at point-blank range. Additional tests were conducted against a fully loaded vehicle from side and rear angles, where penetrations were fully expected to occur. Although the more lightly armoured areas were penetrated by some rounds, the tank did not 'brew-up', and the crew was able to enter the tank and drive it away after mending some track damage. The high level of protection has been achieved not only through the use of advanced armour, but by the use of a sophisticated fire suppression system and compartmentalization of combustibles and ammunition. For example, the ammunition racks at the turret rear are contained behind ready-access panels and, in the event of a detonation of these rounds through battle damage, the compartment has been designed to channel the blast upward through a pair of blast panels in the roof, rather than forward into the crew compartment. The M1 also presents a smaller frontal profile than the bulkier M60.

The US Army plans to acquire 7,000 M1s in the 1980s. Currently under development is the M1E1 version, which will be equipped with the 120mm gun and other features. Other improvements currently under investigation are a CO$_2$ laser rangefinder, which has superior performance in poor weather, a millimetre wave radar for all-weather target acquisition, and a new generation of improved tank ammunition. In testimony before Congress, Army tank officers have expressed confidence in the ability of the M1 to handle new Soviet tank designs such as the projected new T – 80, even if it is fitted with advanced second generation composite armour like the M1. They feel that it will be a less capable design in respect to mobility, fire-on-the-move capability, night fighting and long-range accuracy under all-weather conditions.

The design and testing of the M1 presents a very marked contrast to the ill-fated T95 and MBT – 70 programmes. The M1 was a moderate risk venture with only a modest number of new improved technologies. Such programmes run the risk of design stagnation if innovations are shunned for fear they will compromise the venture due to their excessive cost, complexity or out-and-out failure. To avoid such pitfalls, the Army embarked on a unique test programme called the ACTV (Armoured Combat Test Vehicle) programme to investigate novel tank systems in the fields of suspension, track, engine and transmission design. The HIMAG (High Mobility Agility) vehicle is a specially constructed test bed that can be readily altered to try out new sub-systems in a more cost-effective fashion than modifying a regular production type tank. Similar efforts in the area of light armoured vehicle design are being funded under the HSTV-L (High Survivability Test Vehicle-Light) programme.

BATTLE TANKS

Designation:	M46	M103	M47	T95E1	M48	M48A1	M48A2C	M48A3	M48A5	MBT – 70	M60	M60A1	M60A2	M60A3	M1
Name:	Patton	—	Patton	—	Patton	Patton	Patton	Patton	Patton	—	—	—	—	—	Abrams
Crew:	5	5	5	4	4	4	4	4	4	3	4	4	4	4	4
Loaded weight (kg):	43,999	56,700	46,165	37,739	44,906	47,174	47,174	47,174	48,987	50,400	46,267	48,081	51,982	51,710	54,250
Length overall (cm):	844	1,131	851	1,032	845	872	869	869	943	926	931	944	728	944	977
Length of hull (cm):	635	698	635	688	670	670	670	670	670	730	695	695	695	695	792
Width (cm):	351	376	351	315	363	363	363	363	363	356	363	363	363	363	365
Height (cm):	281	288	296	287	273	313	307	307	328	243	321	326	335	326	237
Production:	c.2,400	200	9,100	11			11,703			14		12,000 +			(7,000?)
Armour (mm)[1]															
glacis:	100	127	100	111	120	120	120	120	120	cl	100 +	100 +	100 +	100 +	450
turret front:	100	127 – 250	100	178	110	110	110	110	110	cl	110	110 +	150 +	110 +	450
turret side:	76	194	63	76	76	76	76	76	76	cl	76	76	76 +	76	450
Main gun:	90mm M3A1	120mm M58	90mm M36	90mm SB	90mm M41	90mm M41	90mm M41	90mm M41	105mm M68	152mm XM150	105mm M68	105mm M68	152mm M162	105mm M68	105mm M68
Elevation:	– 10 + 20°	– 8 + 15°	– 10 + 20°	– 10 + 20°	– 9 + 19°	– 9 + 19°	– 9 + 19°	– 9 + 19°	– 9 + 19°	– 9 + 20°	– 9 + 20°	– 10 + 20°	– 10 + 20°	– 10 + 20°	– 10 + 20°
Rounds stowed:	70	38	71	50	60	60	64	62	54	50	57	63	46	63	55
Coaxial MG:	7.62mm	7.62mm	7.62mm	7.62mm	7.62mm	7.62mm	7.62mm	7.62mm	7.62mm	7.62mm	7.62mm	7.62mm	7.62mm	7.62mm	7.62mm
Secondary armament:	7.62, 12.7mm M2	12.7mm M2	7.62, 12.7mm M2	12.7mm M2	12.7mm M2	12.7mm M2	12.7mm M2	12.7mm M2	12.7mm M2	20mm Mk20	12.7mm M85	12.7mm M85	12.7mm M85	12.7mm M85	7.62, 12.7mm
Rangefinder:	stadia	stereo M15	stereo M12	OPTRAC	stereo M13	stereo M13	stereo M17C	coin M17B1C	coin M17B1C	RL	coin M17C	coin M17A1	RL	RL	Nd:YAG laser
Night vision:	no	no	no	no	no	no	act IR	act IR	act IR	LLLTV	act IR	act IR	act IR	thermal	thermal
IR searchlight:							AN/VSS-1	AN/VSS-2	AN/VSS-2	XSW-30-U	AN/VSS-2	AN/VSS-2	AN/VSS-2	AN/VSS-3A	no
Computer:	no	M14	no		M13	M13	M13A1C	M13A1C	M13A4	yes	M13A1D	M13A2	M19	M21	yes
Stabilization:	no	no	no	no	no	no	no	no	no	yes	no	no	no	yes	yes
Smoke discharger:	no	no	no	no	no	no	no	no	no	yes	no	no	M226	M239	M239
Engine:	AV 1790-5A	AV 1790-5B	AV 1790-5B	AOI 1195-5	AV 1790-5B	AV 1790-5B	AVL 1790-8	AVDS 1790-2A	AVDS 1790-2A	Tele Cont	AVDS 1790-2	AVDS 1790-2A	AVDS 1790-2A	AVDS 1790-2D	AGT-1500
Engine type:	petrol	petrol	petrol	petrol	petrol	petrol	petrol	diesel	diesel	multi	diesel	diesel	diesel	diesel	turbine
Horsepower (hp@rpm):	810@ 2,800	810@ 2,800	810@ 2,800	560@ 2,800	810@ 2,800	810@ 2,800	825@ 2,800	750@ 2,400	750@ 2,400	1450@ 2,600	750@ 2,400	750@ 2,400	750@ 2,400	750@ 2,400	1,500
Power to weight ratio (bhp/tonne):	18.4	14.2	17.5	13.5	18.0	17.1	17.3	15.9	15.9	29.8	16.21	15.31	14.42	14.50	25.1
Transmission:	CD – 850	CD – 850	CD – 850	XTG – 410	CD – 850 – 4	CD – 850 – 4B	CD – 850 – 5	CD – 850	CD – 850	hydro.	CD – 850	CD – 850	CD – 850	CD – 850	X – 110 – 3
Max. speed (km/hr):	59	34	50	56	42	42	50	50	50	72	50	50	50	50	72 (govd.)
cross-country (km/hr):	16	7	14	15	12	12	14	14	14	40	14	14	14	14	50
Max. range (km):	129	129	129	241	112	112	257	463	494	580	499	499	499	499	480
Fuel (litre):	878	1,014	882	757	757	757	1,268	1,420	1,420	1,300	1,457	1,420	1,457	1,457	2,036
Ground pressure (kg/cm^2):	.93	.90	.93	.84	.78	.83	.83	.83	.83	.87	.78	.79	.86	.79	.92

Notes: [1] Armour figures for all vehicles other than the M1 are given in thickness of conventional steel armour; figures for M1 armour are a rough estimate of the equivalent effective thickness of conventional steel armour. **Abbreviations:** act, active; cl, classified data; coin, coincidence; hydro, hydrodynamic; IR, infra-red; LLLTV, low light level television; ND : YAG, Neodymium : Yttrium Aluminium Garnet; RL, ruby laser; SB, stabilized barrel; stadia, stadiametric; stereo, stereoscopic; Tele Cont, Teledyne Continental.

Left: The High Mobility Agility (HIMAG) vehicle is a test bed designed to examine various power plants, fire control systems, suspensions and tracks, without the need to design a whole new vehicle for each test. Here, it is undergoing engine tests at the Yuma Proving Grounds in 1979. (ATAC)

Right, top: During the Second World War, US cavalry units used both armoured cars, such as the M8, and light tanks, such as the M24 Chaffee. The M8 was phased-out after the war, but the M24 remained in service throughout the Korean conflict. Here, a Canadian M8 encounters an Italian M24 during NATO exercises in Italy during August 1951. (US Army)

Right, below: The M41 was a progressive development of the M24 and mounted a more potent 76mm gun. This M41A1 of the 10th Reconnaissance Company, 10th Infantry Division, is covering the advance of an M75 armoured troop carrier in Wurzburg, Germany, during Exercise 'Polo Ball', December 1955. (US Army)

Light Armoured Vehicles

CAVALRY VEHICLES

The rôle of armoured cavalry has traditionally been scouting, flank security, liaison and fast pursuit. During the Second World War, these tasks were fulfilled by three basic types of vehicles: machine-gun armed jeeps, armoured cars and light tanks. The only armoured car used in any number by the US Army was the M8, armed with a 37mm gun in an open turret, and its command version, the machine-gun armed M20. In the light tank category, the M3 and M5 Stuarts were the principal types in service, and in December 1944 the first of the new M24 Chaffee began to enter combat. After the war, the M5A1 Stuart was withdrawn from service in favour of the M24. The US Army, in contrast to many European armies, preferred the light tank in the

reconnaissance rôle, due to its better mobility in rough terrain, snow and mud. Armoured cars were gradually phased-out and were retained only to serve on occupation duty in the US Constabulary. This prejudice against armoured cars has persisted to the present.

The M41 Walker Bulldog Light Tank. The M24 was generally viewed as a satisfactory light tank but, if it had any deficiency, its 75mm gun was viewed as too small to effectively deal with a well armoured adversary. Although the rôle of reconnaissance vehicles was not to battle it out with enemy armour, it was felt prudent to develop a more capable weapon. In 1947, work began on an improved derivative which would incorporate a long-barrelled 76mm gun and a sophisticated stereoscopic range-

finder. This vehicle, the T37, was designed to be air transportable, though few cargo aircraft of the time could easily accommodate so large a load. In 1949, the programme was re-orientated and the complicated rangefinder was dropped as a needless extravagance, resulting in the T41. The T41 formed part of a trio of new tank designs mentioned in the previous chapter, including the T42 medium tank and the T43 heavy tank. The new T41 was to serve as the basis for a whole family of interrelated vehicles, including troop carriers, self-propelled artillery and self-propelled anti-aircraft guns. The T41 was accepted for service use as the M41 Little Bulldog, and the first batch rolled off the assembly line in 1951. It was renamed shortly afterwards as the Walker Bulldog in honour of General Walton H.

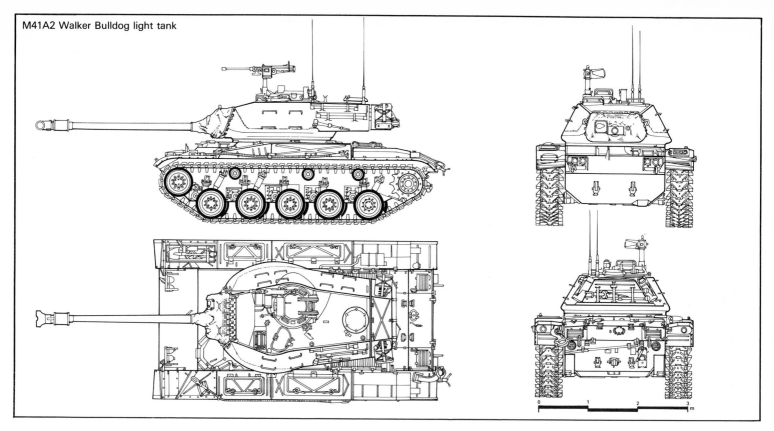

M41A2 Walker Bulldog light tank

Walker who had been killed in an accident in 1950 during the fighting in Korea. Since none of the armoured divisions or armoured cavalry regiments to which the new M41 was assigned served in Korea, it took no part in that conflict. There were 30 M41s assigned to the reconnaissance battalion of each armoured division plus an additional 28 dispersed within the division to headquarters and other units. In 1953, the M41 was replaced on the assembly lines by the M41A1, which used a hydraulic turret traverse in place of the electrical traverse on the older model. The M41 proved to be a popular vehicle in service, with good cross-country speeds compared to other tanks of the period. Its design and layout were fairly conventional, though it did pioneer the use of new hydraulic fire controls which gave it very fast turret traverse. In 1956, new vehicles were fitted with a fuel-injected engine, becoming the M41A2. Field modification kits were issued for the older tanks which, so fitted, were re-designated M41A3.

Besides service in the US Army, the M41 was widely supplied to NATO. It was about half the cost of a current medium tank, and was subsequently offered to many smaller armies in Latin America and the Third World where it has played a visible rôle in several coups. The M41 did not see any significant combat action in American hands, but was the principal tank used by the ARVN during the Vietnam War. In the past decade, there have been a number of modernization efforts to extend the service life of this venerable old design. In the 1950s the US had attempted to up-arm the M41 with a smoothbore, low-pressure 90mm gun as the T49, but dropped the idea. Belgium has developed a version armed with the 90mm low-recoil Cockerill gun, and there have been several re-engining packages offered.

The US Army had hoped to employ the M41 both as the standard cavalry tank and as an air-transportable tank as well. During the war, these tasks had been satisfied by two separate designs, the M22 Locust and the M5A1 Stuart, but the Locust airborne tank was not entirely successful. The problem was that the M41 was really too large to be air-dropped and was a very awkward vehicle to transport by air. Reluctantly, the Army began studies of smaller tanks which could be used in air-assault operations. Two proposals were examined in 1952. The Cadillac T71 was a small, eighteen-ton light tank of fairly conventional layout armed with a

76mm gun and with armour not exceeding 35mm. In contrast, the T92 developed by AAI was of very peculiar appearance with a cleft turret, self-contained 76mm gun and twin machine-gun sub-turrets positioned toward the rear of the tank's hull. Prototypes of the T92 entered trials in 1957, but by this date it was recognized that the 76mm gun was not really adequate to deal with contemporary Soviet tanks, and the M56 Scorpion had proved satisfactory, even if not fully armoured.

The M114. The main problem of using only light tanks in the cavalry rôle is that they are quite costly, and in many cases are extravagant for many of the less demanding tasks. In 1956, the Army started development of a new tracked vehicle to serve alongside the M41 (and later M551) in much the same fashion as the M20 had been used in the Second World War. The vehicle's design criteria called for light weight to allow it to be used as an air-transportable troop carrier, and some thought was also given to using it as a battalion recoilless rifle

carrier in place of the M50 Ontos project that the Army had rejected. A wheeled recoilless rifle/personnel carrier, the T115, was built, but quickly fell from favour in the face of the T114 tracked carrier. With the advent of new, wire-guided anti-tank missiles, such as the SS – 11 and ENTAC, questions were raised about the longevity of the recoilless rifle concept. The T114 was better configured for the command and reconnaissance rôle, and various armament options were considered, including a small machine-gun armed turret. The Army settled on a simpler version armed with a .50 calibre machine-gun on an exposed pintle mount and an M60 machine-gun at the rear. These first entered service in 1961 as the M114; 619 were built.

The M114's resemblance to a shrunken M113 has often created confusion over its lineage. It is not in fact related to the M113, which was developed by FMC, but was a wholly independent design developed by DDAD/GM. A more striking dissimilarity to

the M113 was its lack of success in Army service. Although the M114 was a fairly conventional design, it proved to be a failure. It was unreliable, and had particular difficulty extracting itself from river banks or other steep grades, and it had poor traction in mud. These mobility problems were especially undesirable in a scout vehicle, and first became evident when the M114 was introduced into ARVN armoured cavalry units. Their American advisers insisted that the M114 be replaced by the larger but more manoeuvrable M113, but these problems were not appreciated and the M114 was introduced into service with American units in Europe. A modified version, the M114A1, was introduced in 1963 but had no chassis improvements. Rather, the exposed .50 calibre machine-gun was replaced by a new mounting which allowed it to be fired from within the vehicle. A total of 3,095 of these were manufactured, with the first 1,295 using a hand cupola traverse and subsequent vehicles using a power traverse. It was felt that the .50 calibre was

Left, top: The M41 was the standard tank of the South Vietnamese Army throughout the war, though it was supplemented by some M48A3s in the concluding years of the conflict. This M41A2 of the 1st ARVN Cavalry Regiment has been fitted with a VSS – 2 infra-red searchlight and an improvised armour shield over the commander's .50 calibre M2 machine-gun. (James Loop)

Left, below: For a time, consideration was given to adopting a small light tank for the airborne divisions, and the T92 developed by AAI was tested. It was a unique vehicle of very unconventional design, but the programme was dropped since it was felt that the M56 already in service offered better firepower and lower weight. (Steven Zaloga)

Above: The M114 was adopted as a reconnaissance vehicle to bridge the gap between expensive light tanks and poorly-protected scout jeeps. Unfortunately, serious mobility shortcomings condemned the M114 to failure and it was phased out in the late 1970s. Here an M114A1 serving with the Armored Cavalry Platoon, 2/54th Infantry of the 4th Armored Division, takes part in exercises near Grafenwohr, Germany. (US Army)

Right: The initial version of the M114 series used as its primary armament a .50 calibre M2 machine-gun on an exposed mount. Subsequent models used a remote control mount. This M114 of the 3rd Platoon, C Troop, 4/12th Cavalry, is on exercises at Fort Carson, Colorado, in September 1969. It is marked prominently with the cavalry guidon insignia.

inadequate to deal with Soviet light armoured vehicles such as the BTR – 50 and BTR – 60, so in 1967 the M114s and M114A1s began to be re-armed with an M139 20mm cannon on a remote-control mount to permit its firing by the crew from inside. The vehicles re-armed with this Hispano-Suiza cannon were redesignated M114A2. The cannon proved to be as cantankerous as the rest of the vehicle and, in 1973, General Creighton Abrams finally labelled it a failure. It was gradually replaced by the M113 until a more satisfactory vehicle could be developed. Ironically, FMC meanwhile had developed a cut-down version of their popular M113, sometimes called the M113½, to fulfil this same rôle. This was adopted by the Canadian Army as the Lynx, and also served with success in the Dutch and Belgian armies. Many M114s were sold to vehicle collectors or for scrap, but some were retained for test use and about fifty were converted by Emerson Electronics for the Air Force to serve as radar simulators with electronic equipment mounted on the roof. These are called TRTG (Tactical Radar Threat Generator) and simulate the B – 76 (Gun Dish) radar on the ZSU – 23 – 4 Shilka.

The M551 Sheridan. The flurry of light armoured vehicle projects in the 1950s did not conclude the Army's search for a vehicle which could fulfil both the airborne and cavalry rôles, so in 1961 a new programme was launched which would prove to be the most ambitious and controversial yet. In keeping with the Department of Defense's fondness for convoluted acronyms, the new vehicle was christened the Armoured Reconnaissance/Airborne Assault Vehicle (AR/AAV) XM551, and Army officials were quite insistent that it should not be called a light tank. The problem faced by previous cavalry/airborne tanks was that the cavalry requirement for respectable firepower directly contradicted the airborne call for a lightweight chassis. The larger the gun, the greater the recoil, and hence the greater the need for a heavy chassis to absorb the shock of the recoil. Recoilless rifles were out of the question in view of the limitations in their armoured vehicle applications, and while the new wire-guided anti-tank missiles offered several desirable qualities, they were not really suitable for close support against unarmoured targets. A revolutionary advance in tank armament was needed to break this vicious circle. The Army thought it had found the necessary breakthrough in the form of an unconventional gun/missile launcher, which was to be mounted on the new tank. In contrast to earlier light tanks, it was to be armoured with aluminium rather than steel and be fully amphibious. This was a very ambitious package indeed.

The new gun/missile launcher was centred on the Ford Shillelagh guided anti-tank missile. The missile was fired from the gun tube at subsonic speeds, at which point a solid-fuel motor boosted the missile to an impressive 1,100m/sec. The missile contained a small infra-red tracker in the tail which, at about 1,200m after launch, picked up a signal from a transmitter located above the gun barrel. The gunner kept the target in his sights, and the infra-red transmitter automatically fed course adjustments to the missile. Such a system was accurate beyond three kilometres, but had a dead zone under 1,000 metres. The warhead was a potent 6.8kg shaped-charge, which was sufficient to destroy any existing tank it detonated against. While these features were radical enough on their own, the XM81 gun/launcher also fired several different types of conventional rounds that employed consumable cases. In contrast to a conventional gun, which uses ammunition fired from reusable brass cases, once the XM81 had fired one of its rounds, there was no need to eject the spent case since it had been consumed when the propellant launched the projectile.

This novel gun/launcher system was also adopted on the XM66 and MBT – 70 and soon became the source of serious technical problems that delayed all three tank programmes. The Shillelagh proved less accurate than anticipated and, while on tropical trials, only two of thirteen rounds hit the target. This was especially frightening, since each round cost about $13,000 at the time or about as much as a

M551 Sheridan Armoured Reconnaissance/Airborne Assault Vehicle

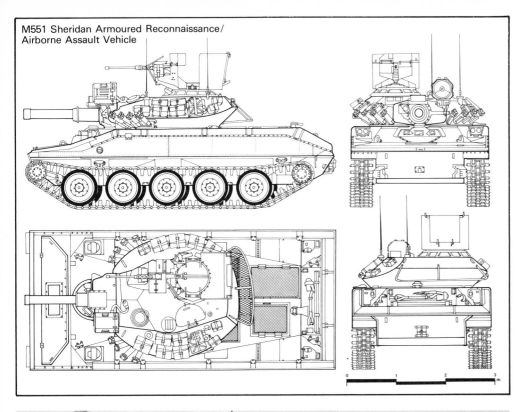

Rolls Royce. In spite of unresolved technical problems, the Army rushed the Sheridan into production in 1966 for fear that Congress would cut funding. Serious as the problems with the guided missile rounds were, far more disturbing troubles cropped up with the conventional rounds. The caseless ammunition was very fragile, and a sharp rap on the case was sometimes sufficient to split it open, spilling explosive propellant on the turret basket floor. The caseless ammunition liner absorbed moisture and in these circumstances the propellant case was not entirely consumed when fired, leaving smouldering débris in the breech which had a nasty habit of prematurely 'cooking off' the subsequent round, occasionally before the breech was closed, causing easily imaginable havoc inside the turret. The Army was committed to using caseless ammunition, since the MBT–70 automatic loader could not accommodate a change to conventional brass-cased ammunition without substantial re-design. In 1966 and 1967, several fixes were tried, including the use of a neoprene or nylon storage bag for the caseless ammunition and an open breech scavenger system to blow débris out of the gun tube by air pressure. The Australian Army tested the Sheridan in 1967 and 1968 but found it unacceptable for use in a Vietnam-type environment due to unsuitable ammunition, unreliable missile rounds, ineffective scavenger system, inadequate engine cooling and the fragility of the gunner's periscope. It was found that the missile round did not cause any undue problems for the gunner, but that the effects of conventional rounds were so severe that they propelled the whole tank back two or three feet, threatening injury to the crew unless they were braced for the blast. It created havoc with the carefully bore-sighted optical sights and laser rangefinder. These problems also plagued the XM66/M60A2 and MBT–70 programmes, as mentioned in the earlier chapter.

With several hundred tanks on its hands not durable enough for troop use, the Army embarked on a crash improvement programme. The Army was especially anxious to try out the Sheridan in Vietnam, in the hope that a good showing there would placate Congressional critics. A canister round was developed specially for use in Vietnam since the regular anti-tank rounds would be of little use. In January 1969, the tanks for the first two squadrons were sent to Vietnam for trials with the 4th Cavalry and 11th Armored Cavalry. The deployment was premature and, rather than helping to mollify critics, only provided them with added reason to question the Army's handling of the programme. The cavalry troops in Vietnam really did not need the Sheridan since the M113 ACAV (Armoured Cavalry Assault Vehicle) had proved so successful, and the heavier M48 Patton was more than adequate whenever a heavily armoured vehicle with firepower was required. The Sheridan was disliked not only because of teething problems with the main gun, but also because of engine overheating and the incessant whine of its superchargers. It was particularly sensitive to mine damage, which was exacerbated by the tank crews' preference for stowing large quantities of machine-gun ammunition rather than the troublesome caseless type. The canister round proved savagely effective against infantry; one night-time tactic was to move a Sheridan near a Vietcong infiltration route under observation with the use of an infra-red searchlight. Once the enemy column was near, the canister round was fired with grim results. Several fixes were adopted in Vietnam, including the substitution of a closed breech scavenger system for the troublesome open breech model, the addition of underpan armour below the driver, and the fabrication of an armoured 'crow's nest' around the commander's cupola to protect the crewman firing the roof .50 calibre machine-gun.

After much sweat and frustration, the M551 was finally judged suitable for service use and was shipped to units in Europe to replace both the M41 and the M56. The M551 was more suitable for the European environment since its main advantage, its tremendous anti-tank firepower, was really not appropriate to the type of anti-guerrilla war fought in

Left, top: The M114A1 was the most heavily armed version of the series, but the M139 20mm gun proved cantankerous in service.
Left, middle: Although not adopted by the US Army, a smaller version of the M113 was developed by FMC to fill the same rôle as the ill-fated M114. In Canadian service it is called the Lynx, while the Dutch version (pictured here), armed with a 25mm Oerlikon autocannon, is called the M113 C&R. (Dutch Army via George Balin)
Left, below: The Army was anxious to test the Sheridan tank in combat and, at the end of 1968, the first batch of M551 arrived in Vietnam. The 11th Armored Cavalry was one of the first two units to receive these vehicles. One of their vehicles, nicknamed 'The Devil Avenges', is seen here, photographed by one of the authors at Bien Hoa in January 1969.
Middle: The M551 was not as popular in Vietnam as the Patton or the M113, and its light frame was particularly susceptible to mine damage. This vehicle, belonging to A Company of 1/1st Cavalry, Americal Division, in operation near Tam Ky on 18 March 1970, has the field modification armour kit added under the bow to protect the driver from mine blast. (US Army)
Bottom: The Sheridan was fully amphibious and used a self-contained fabric flotation collar to provide enough freeboard to float. Here an M551 of the 4/9th Cavalry exits from the bank of the Kyle River during exercises at Fort Campbell, Kentucky, in May 1968. The 4/9th was among the first cavalry units to be equipped with the Sheridan. (US Army)

Vietnam. The temperate climate was kinder to the sensitive caseless ammunitiion, though problems caused by the severe gun recoil continued to plague both the M551 and the M60A2. Although cantankerous and with a certain fragility, no other seventeen-ton tank has equalled the combined mobility and firepower of the Sheridan. In addition to its use as a scout vehicle, the M551 was also deployed with airborne units. The usual method of air-dropping is called low-altitude extraction. The Sheridan is mounted on a fibreboard platform with a drogue chute at the rear. The transport aircraft approaches the drop zone as low as safety will permit, and the drogue chute is deployed, pulling the tank out of the rear. The pallet absorbs most of the impact as the tank careens along the ground. The crew is parachuted in, and once they reach the tank, they unfasten the pallet and drive off.

The M551 served until 1979, by which time it was being replaced in the armoured cavalry units by M113s and M60s. These will be superseded in turn when the new M3 Cavalry Fighting Vehicle becomes available. The only unit still retaining the M551 is the tank battalion of the 82nd Airborne Division, though about 300 are in use with OPFOR's training units and as test beds for the ACVT programme. The remaining M551s remain in storage for possible use at a later date as a carrier for electronic jamming equipment. For example, AAI has developed a number of possible new armament packages for the Sheridan, including conventional 76mm and 90mm guns, but there has been no commitment yet from the Army on the fate of this project. There have been indications recently (July 1981) that 1,000 Sheridans are to be sold to South Korea, presumably to be re-armed and re-built. The definitive replacement for the M551, the M3 CFV, was developed as part of the search for a new armoured personnel carrier. It is basically a close derivative of the M2 Infantry Fighting Vehicle, and is covered in more detail on page 56.

In view of the failure of the M114 reconnaissance vehicle and the continuing problems with the M551 AR/AAV, in 1971 the Army initiated the XM800 ARSV (Armoured Reconnaissance Scout Vehicle) programme. The aim was to develop a lightweight scout armed with a 20mm cannon and fitted with a wide range of sophisticated observation gear, such as passive night sights and a small surveillance radar. The vehicle was to be fully amphibious with high cross-country speed, and both wheeled and tracked configurations were considered. The competition narrowed down to two entries, a tracked vehicle from FMC and a wheeled vehicle from Lockheed. The FMC entry was a conventional light tank with aluminium hull armour and a fully rotating turret. It had provision for a three-man crew. The Lockheed entry was an offshoot of their earlier XM808 Twister articulated armoured car, which had been sent to Vietnam for experimental trials. The Lockheed XM800 was very unconventional in appearance owing to its articulated frame, but was fully amphibious. Irrespective of the technical merits of either design, in 1975 the ARSV programme was abandoned. The ARSV was rapidly becoming as complex and expensive as the existing M551 AR/AAV and the Department of Defense and Congress insisted that the whole scout vehicle programme be reassessed.

Part of the growing confusion over the reconnaissance vehicle programme was caused by the changing tactical needs of the Army. The US experience in Vietnam had made the Army enthusiastic proponents of helicopters, especially in the reconnaissance rôle. Their mobility was far superior to that of tactical vehicles, though of course they could not perform all the duties required in that rôle, such as flank security or under certain weather conditions. Several commercial firms independently developed reconnaissance vehicles with private funds and tried to win Army acceptance of their ideas. FMC developed the XR311 which was in essence a souped-up Baja dune buggy.

In 1977 the cavalry vehicle picture took on more clarity. The resuscitation of the MICV (Mechanized Infantry Combat Vehicle) infantry vehicle

Top: After service in Vietnam, the Sheridan-equipped 4th Cavalry served with the Seventh Army in Germany, an environment that proved far better suited to the M551. This M551 belonged to the 1/4th Cavalry and was photographed near Grafenwohr in April 1976. It sports the Seventh Army-style camouflage scheme and is fitted with an armoured crow's nest to protect the commander when using the external machine-gun. (Brian Gibbs)

Middle: Among the most radical new light tank designs is the HSTV-L test bed, developed by AAI and fielded for trials in 1979. This futuristic vehicle is built around a revolutionary 75mm Ares automatic cannon firing telescoped ammunition at a rate of one round per second. AAI is currently developing a two-man derivative as a possible contender for both the Marine MPWS competition and Army requirements. In 1980 work began on a larger version with a 90mm gun. (AAI Corporation)

Below: The Army experimented with articulated wheeled vehicle suspensions in the 1960s. Among the armoured test beds for this technology was the Lockheed XM808 Twister, shown here during trials in Vietnam in 1970. It was armed with a remote control 20mm M139, similar to that used on the later models of the M114. (US Army)

Right, top: Although the M60 was not used in Vietnam, two M60 variants saw service there: the M60 (AVLB) bridgelayer and the M728 combat engineer vehicle, which is pictured here serving with the 1st Infantry Brigade, 5th Mechanized Infantry Division, near Quang Tri in August 1968. (US Army)

Right, below: The first combat use of the Sheridan AR/AAV took place at the end of 1968 and in early 1969 with the 4th Cavalry and 11th Armored Cavalry in Vietnam. The vehicle shown here belonged to Troop D of 3/4th Cavalry and served in support of the 25th Infantry Division in February 1969. (US Army)

programme led the Department of Defense to instruct the Army to co-ordinate its cavalry and infantry needs on a single vehicle, the XM723. The resulting vehicle would serve as a replacement for both the M114 and the M551. This eventually materialized as the M3 Cavalry Fighting Vehicle (see page 56). The pendulum has again swung away from a high-low mix of two different cavalry vehicles, back to a state where a single vehicle is to serve as the cavalry reconnaissance vehicle. There was to be one final quirk in the sweep of the pendulum. In 1977 the Army planned to develop a light armoured vehicle under the Combat Support Vehicle programme. The aim was somewhat hazy, as the vehicle described by the Army requirement was in some respects another attempt to find a lightly armoured weapons carrier for infantry anti-tank teams (this time carrying the TOW missile launcher instead of the 106mm recoilless rifle) but also suitable as a reconnaissance vehicle. This ambiguity was evident in the industry response: Cadillac Gage's vehicle was clearly aimed at the latter requirement, while FMC's re-designed XR311 with light Kevlar armour was configured mainly for the weapons carrier rôle. In any event, Congress was unhappy with the proliferation of Army vehicle programmes and refused to fund the XM966 CSV effort. Eventually, it was resurrected in 1979 as the High Mobility Multi-Purpose Wheeled Vehicle, but this time the intention was clear to develop a lightly armoured weapons carrier for infantry, airborne and air-mobile anti-tank teams as well as unarmoured versions for other rôles usually fulfilled by M151 jeeps and light trucks. The central aim of the programme is to develop a new light truck to replace older vehicles, such as the M151 and M561 Gamma Goat, rather than a new wheeled cavalry reconnaissance vehicle.

ARMOURED CARS

The US Army has never had much sympathy for armoured cars, even if they are widely employed by most other armies. Aside from the ill-fated T115 and Lockheed XM808 Twister, there have been no other major armoured car types developed on US Army initiative since the Second World War. Nevertheless, there have been several armoured cars developed by commercial firms, in the United States, mainly aimed at the export market. The most successful of these has been the Cadillac Gage Commando series.

The Commando Series. Although not as mobile in rough or soft terrain as tracked vehicles, armoured cars are only a fraction of the cost of tracked vehicles, are easier to maintain, are more reliable and consume less fuel. This makes them especially attractive to small nations with modest budgets, and especially to those countries which use their armies mainly as internal security forces. Such vehicles are also popular for security work, for example convoy protection, in time of war. In the early 1960s, Cadillac Gage, whose prior military experience had been primarily in the design of tank fire control systems, embarked on an independent programme to develop a simple armoured car, using commonly available commercial parts, which would offer good mobility and be fully amphibious. Their first product was the V–100 Commando, a four-wheel drive vehicle the size of a lorry. It was offered with a variety of light armament packages, either turreted machine-guns, exposed pulpit mounts, or lightly armed troop transport versions. It was mainly intended for troop transport or security duties. Civil versions were offered, including a police riot control version and even an unarmoured amphibious fire lorry. The military versions were designed to withstand 7.62mm ball ammunition. The V–100 interested the US Army, which had found itself without a suitable security vehicle for use in Vietnam. Convoys were being escorted by armed jeeps and lorries, but were suffering heavy casualties. The Military Police (MP) had begun to build improvized armoured cars on jeep and lorry chassis. In 1966, a small batch of V–100s were purchased for trials and were called XM706 in Army service. The Army recommended a number of small

Left, top: An M113 ACAV of the 9th Infantry Division enters a stream near the perimeter of Fire Base Bastogne in Vietnam, 16 April 1968. The bow plane is locked down to prevent water from washing over the roof while the vehicle is in the stream. (US Army)
Left, below: This view of an M56 Scorpion of D Company, 16th Armor, arriving at Bien Hoa in June 1965, shows quite clearly how little armour protected this vehicle. Nevertheless, it packed a large 90mm gun and was very light. (US Army)
Top: The Lockheed entry in the ill-fated XM800 ARSV programme during the mid 1970s was this intriguing wheeled armoured car, which was derived from their experiences on the XM808 project. It was armed with a 25mm cannon, although it is absent from this vehicle which currently rests in the museum grounds at Aberdeen Proving Grounds. (Steven Zaloga)
Middle: The FMC entry in the XM800 ARSV programme was a small amphibious tank with a three-man crew. This pilot vehicle was provided with a sophisticated array of sensors to carry out scouting missions, as was the Lockheed entry. (FMC Corporation)
Below: The Commando series of armoured cars has been among the most successful and numerous produced since 1945. Several hundred of the initial V–100 version were used by the ARVN for convoy escort duty during the Vietnam War. This particular vehicle is one of the initial batch of XM706 armed with .50 calibre and .30 calibre machine-guns. The initial batch did not have a Molotov cocktail shield over the engine grilles in the roof, and the driver's hatches were flat. (James Loop)

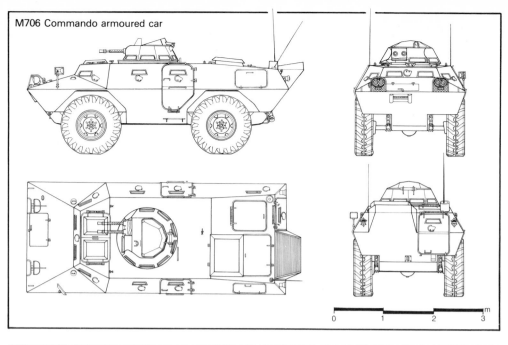

M706 Commando armoured car

changes which were incorporated in later batches. The definitive M706 was bought in larger numbers and, in June 1967, arrived in Vietnam to serve with the 540th and 720th Military Police Battalions to provide convoy escort. Several hundred were eventually purchased for use by both the US Army and the ARVN. The M706, popularly called 'Ducks' by the MPs due to their pointed prows, were well received and soon became heavily involved in the fighting along the hazardous convoy routes. The first batch of XM706 up to serial 10619 had flat, driver's hatches and no Molotov cocktail shield over the upper engine grille. The later batch of XM706 were fitted with raised hatches for the driver, shields, and several other small improvements. These vehicles could be fitted with a variety of machine-guns, the usual armament being a pair of .30 calibre machine-guns or one .30 calibre and one .50 calibre machine-gun. The definitive M706 incorporated all of the improvements mentioned but was designed only to fit the twin M73 .30 calibre machine-guns. Most of the Commandos used by the US Army were the M706 version, though the ARVN did use the XM706. The success of the M706 in US Army service led the Air Force to purchase Commandos for airfield security duty. The Air Force version was the XM706E2 which had, in place of a turret, a lightly armoured parapet with folding pintle mounts that could accommodate a variety of machine-guns. The military was not the only American user of the V–100. Several city police forces purchased Commandos for riot control in the wake of urban rioting during the tense summer months of the mid 1960s.

The V–100 proved to be a commercial success overseas as well. The largest single user was the ARVN with over 400 XM706 and M706. After the fall of South Vietnam, these vehicles served with the Vietnamese Army in the war with China and Cambodia. The V–100 is in use with both military forces and police units in eleven countries. An unlicensed copy is built in Portugal as the 'Chaimite'. Foreign clients expressed interest in a more heavily armed version of the V–100 that could accommodate an automatic cannon or a low-recoil anti-tank gun. This led to the V–200 in 1969, which closely resembles the V–100, though it is a much heavier vehicle. It was sold to Singapore. The V–200 was not as well received as the earlier V–100, and Cadillac Gage decided to develop an improved V–100 which bridged the gap between these two previous Commando models. This was unveiled in 1971 as the V–150. It most closely resembles the V–100 but was modified to allow it to mount power turrets with a gun as large as the Cockerill 90mm. It soon proved to be the most successful member of the Commando family. Over twenty-two countries now use the Commando series in some twenty different models. One of the main attractions of the V–150 was the wide range of armament options offered with it. This feature enabled an army to purchase a fleet of interrelated vehicles, some configured as troop carriers, others as scouts, and so on, all sharing common automotive spares. Total production of the Commando series is not known but is believed to exceed 3,600 vehicles, making it the world's most widely manufactured armoured car since 1945, with the probable exception of the Soviet BTR–60. The different versions include cannon-armed versions with the Model 204GK Oerlikon 20mm autocannon, the 90mm Cockerill gun, an APC version for twelve troops, a version with a twin machine-gun turret similar to that used on the M706, another machine-gun version with a one metre turret for mounting heavier machine-guns, an 81mm mortar version, a turreted version with a 76mm gun similar to that used on the Scorpion light tank, a command version with pod roof, a recovery version with a jib boom, a police emergency rescue version, a base security vehicle comparable to the XM706E2, and an air defence version with an 20mm Vulcan Gatling gun. Besides the basic versions, there are other turret options, including one mounting an automatic 40mm grenade launcher. In 1979, Cadillac Gage introduced an enlarged Commando, the V–300 based on a 6×6 chassis as compared to the 4×4

Left, middle: The M706 'Duck' was the principal version of the V–100 series used for convoy escort and base security duties by the US Military Police in Vietnam. This vehicle, 'Iron Man', served with the 66th Military Police Company. The use of colourful cartoons from the Marvel Superheroes comics were very common on MP armoured cars during the war. (US Army)

Left, below: The Air Force used the XM706E2 version of the Commando series in Vietnam for base security and perimeter defence. This version had a small, open parapet on the roof with folding armoured doors insead of a turret. The XM706E2 shown here is in action at Phan Rang Air Base in Vietnam, June 1969. (USAF)

Right, top: The most recent addition to the Commando series is the large V–300. This version has rear exit doors and, in common with other versions of the Commando, can be equipped with a variety of turrets. (Cadillac Gage)

Right, middle: Chrysler developed several armoured cars for export in the 1960s, but the only type produced in quantity was the MAC–1, which was sold in small numbers to Mexico for security duty. (Chrysler Defense Division)

Below: The most widely exported version of the Commando series to date has been the V–150 series. This vehicle, of the 20mm turret type, was the version supplied to Saudi Arabia for the mechanization of their National Guard. (Cadillac Gage)

Above: Cadillac Gage developed the small, two-man Scout to compete in the CSV programme but, when the programme was abandoned, the future of the vehicle was left in limbo. Subsequently, the firm developed several versions of the Scout independently, including one with a TOW launcher, for possible export. (Cadillac Gage)

Middle: Arrowpointe developed the Dragoon 300 series of armoured cars for the export market in the late 1970s. This particular model is equipped with a low-pressure 90mm Cockerill gun of Belgian design. (Arrowpointe Corp.)

Below: The Hydracobra is an Americanized version of a Brazilian Engesa armoured car that was developed by Bell Aerospace as an entry in the Marine LAV programme.

Right, top: The Army is currently developing, under the HMWC programme, a light truck which will also be manufactured in a lightly armoured version (shown here) and equipped with a TOW missile launcher. This particular vehicle is the XM966 entry from FMC. (FMC)

Right, middle: The Air Force has begun to purchase these small, lightly armoured Peacekeeper lorries for base security. They will also be acquired by the Department of Energy to guard nuclear plants. (Cadillac Gage)

Right, below: The Mowag Piranha is manufactured by GM Canada. A version mounting an AAI universal turret armed with an Ares 75mm automatic cannon was submitted as a contender in the Marine LAV programme.

chassis used on the V – 150. The re-design has permitted several improvements, most notably the use of large rear doors for troop exit.

The Dragoon and Peacekeeper. Although Cadillac Gage has been the most successful exporter of armoured cars in the United States, there have been other firms working in the field. In 1963 Chrysler developed a conventional 4 × 4 type, called the MAC – 1 (Medium Armoured Car – 1) armed with a 20mm gun, of which forty were sold to Mexico where it is known as the MEX – 1. Several other armament options were proposed but never materialized, and an improved type, the MAC – 2, was undertaken for manufacture by Chrysler España for the Guardia Civil. Similarly, other efforts by the firm, such as their light armoured car and SWAT vehicle, never reached production. Another firm in the field is Arrowpointe, who offer the Dragoon 300. This was initially offered by AM General as the AM – 300 in 1978. The Dragoon is similar in size and configuration to the V – 150 and, like its competitor, is offered with different armament packages. It is built around existing military lorry components, and uses the same engine as the M113A1.

The possibility of the US armed forces adopting an armoured car for combat rôles not limited to security duties appears far more likely with the advent of the Rapid Deployment Force. The Iranian crisis in 1980 focused attention on the lack of light armoured vehicles suitable for rapid airlifting to crisis centres. Moreover, an examination of Marine unit organization found that their capabilities for speedy assaults beyond the immediate beach area were quite limited due to the lack of sufficient armoured equipment. These evaluations spawned the LAV (Light Armoured Vehicle) programme, which aims at adapting an existing light armoured vehicle to Marine needs. The basic version would be a troop carrier armed with a 25mm Bushmaster cannon, and there would be a family of related support types, including an assault gun version armed with a low-pressure gun in the 76mm – 90mm range. A number of vehicles have been proposed for these requirements, including the V – 300, an Americanized-version of the Engesa Casceval, the British Scorpion tank, and the Canadian Grizzly and Cougar armoured cars. A small number of the latter were leased by the USMC for desert trials to examine the feasibility of the LAV concept in 1980. It is expected that a LAV production vehicle will be selected in 1982 and that about 700 will be built. The Army is currently reconsidering its own needs for light armoured cars under the LAWCV programme (Light Armoured Wheeled Combat Vehicle). The Marines are also considering a more sophisticated light armoured vehicle under the MPWS (Mobile Protected Weapon System) programme, which will presumably be a light tracked vehicle developed primarily for the anti-armour rôle.

While the prospects for a combat oriented American armoured car are still cloudy, the picture is different regarding security vehicles. In 1980, the Air Force began receiving the first of its new Peacekeeper security vehicles. The Peacekeeper vehicle was developed to fulfil an Air Force and Department of Energy requirement for a small, lightly armoured security vehicle for base patrol. Several automotive firms offered competitive designs, with the contract going to Cadillac Gage. The Peacekeeper is a small 4 × 4 based on a Dodge W – 300 light truck chassis that can be fitted with a small machine-gun turret. It has small firing ports on either side and the rear, and is being used by airfield patrols as well as guards at nuclear facilities, though some military officials question the Peacekeeper's ability to withstand mine or small arms damage.

TANK DESTROYERS

The demise of the Tank Destroyer Command in 1945 and certain technological advances led to the disappearance of tracked tank destroyers in the US Army. Recoilless rifles could be mounted easily on jeeps to provide the infantry with cheap, mobile anti-tank firepower. In armoured and mechanized divisions, main battle tanks fulfilled the functions of medium and heavy tanks as well as tank destroyers. In the 1950s, wire-guided anti-tank missiles such as Dart, SS – 11 and ENTAC began to attract attention, and some were experimentally fitted to tanks and M59 APCs. However, no dedicated anti-tank vehicle resulted from these trials. The M50 Ontos and the M56 Scorpion were the closest the services came to adopting a conventional tank destroyer.

The M56 Scorpion. The M56 had been developed by the Army to provide airborne divisions with a measure of anti-tank firepower. The prime requirement for the vehicle was extremely light weight to allow it to be easily air dropped. As a result, armour protection was minimal. The M54 90mm gun was mounted centrally on the vehicle with only a thin shield in front of the gun. Ammunition was stowed immediately below the gun. The first M56 Scorpions

came off the production lines in 1953 and were deployed with the 82nd and 101st Airborne Divisions. The M56 weighed only about half as much as the T92 airborne tank, which was under development at the time, and only about a quarter of the M41 light tank, yet had heavier firepower than either. In fact, the large gun proved a problem in action, since the recoil severely shook the small chassis, and the proximity of the barrel to the ground raised thick clouds of dust in front of the Scorpion. Usually, the gun commander would remain away from the vehicle when firing to better observe the target and call corrections. It remained in service through the Vietnam War, serving with the 173rd Airborne to provide fire support. It had more firepower than its Soviet counterpart, the ASU – 57, but many of the same shortcomings, and was eventually withdrawn in favour of the M551 Sheridan which finally succeeded in mating the rôles of cavalry vehicle and airborne tank in one vehicle.

The abolition of Tank Destroyer Command after the war did not negate the need for small, mobile anti-tank weapons and, in 1952, a further light armoured vehicle project was initiated. There was some interest in designing a better-protected carrier than jeeps for the anti-tank teams, and a tracked weapons carrier was built for trials. The new tracked carrier, mounting six recoilless rifles, was satisfactory, but the Army decided its needs were satisfied by existing jeeps. However, the Marines were looking for a light armoured vehicle to replace their ageing Sherman tanks. The USMC was in the midst of a restructuring aimed at giving the Corps greater strategic mobility, and ease of transport was a prime requisite. As a result, the recoilless rifle carrier entered production in 1955 as the M50 Ontos. The name Ontos, Greek for 'The Thing', was certainly appropriate, given the ungainly appearance of the M50. The M50 was introduced into Marine service in 1956, with 45 serving in each divisional tank battalion.

The M50 Ontos. The Ontos was one of the least conventional armoured vehicles to enter service during this period. The hull, derived from the T55/T56 APC, was very thinly armoured and

resembled a pyramid topped with a small circular cupola. Several armament arrangements were developed, but an array of six 106mm recoilless rifles was selected. Stalks jutted out from the cupola on either side to which were attached a cluster of three recoilless rifles. The crew consisted of a driver, loader and a commander/gunner. The fire controls were rudimentary, and ranging was accomplished through the use of a spotting rifle mounted over each cluster of recoilless rifles. Once the target had been acquired and the guns laid, the commander fired the spotting rifle and watched the path of the tracer round. If it struck the target, the rifles were fired. All six rifles could be fired simultaneously, which created an awesome backblast of gas, but since only eighteen rounds were carried it was prudent to fire only one rifle at a time. Recoilless rifles have obvious advantages for light armoured vehicles, since they enable a very small tank to carry a weapon with impressive firepower and anti-armour penetration with very little recoil. A vehicle such as the Ontos could never stand up to the recoil forces of a conventional, tubed gun with performance akin to the 106mm recoilless rifle. However, there are also obvious drawbacks. The enormous backblast of gas from the weapon quickly attracts attention which, in view of the vehicle's thin armour, could prove fatal; also, because of the backblast of gas, recoilless rifles have to be mounted externally, and therefore reloaded each time outside the protective armour of the tank. This latter fault was especially evident in Vietnam, where snipers were a real hazard to crews reloading their guns.

The M50 saw combat in 1965 with the 6th Marines in the Dominican Republic. The Dominican rebels had a handful of old Landsverk L – 60 light tanks that had been purchased as 'agricultural tractors', as well as a few AMX – 13s. Several of these were knocked out during the sporadic fighting. The Ontos was more widely used in Vietnam, but it was not well suited to this type of anti-guerrilla rôle. Its single machine-gun was carried externally in a very exposed position, and its thin armour was very susceptible to mines. The Ontos was phased-out in favour of tanks, but, ironically, in 1980 the Marines

Left, below: The M56's only major combat tour took place with Company D, 16th Armor, 173rd Airborne Brigade, in Vietnam, where it was commonly called the SPAT (for self-propelled anti-tank gun). Here, an M56 from the company fires at a Vietcong position during Operation 'Toledo' on 17 July 1967. (US Army)

Right and below: The M50 Ontos, which was used to provide fire support for Marine amphibious assaults, could produce an awesome display of firepower from its six 106mm recoilless rifles, but it was not entirely successful in Vietnam. The top photograph shows an Ontos of A Company, 1st Anti-Tank Battalion, 1st Marine Division, moving through coastal sand dunes during Operation 'Mobile', Vietnam, May 1966. In the photograph below, an M50 shepherds a pair of the ungainly LVTP–5 AmTracs of the 9th Marine Amphibious Brigade during Operation 'Deckhouse VI', Vietnam, February 1967. (USMC)

LIGHT ARMOURED VEHICLES

Designation:	M41A2	M114A1	M551	HSTV-L	M706	V–150	V–200	V–300	—	—	M50	M56
Name:	Walker Bulldog		Sheridan	—	Duck	Commando	Commando	Commando	Peacekeeper	Dragoon 300	Ontos	Scorpion
Production:	5,500	3,714	1,729		10	4	9	4	5	9	240 (3)	
Crew:	4	3	4	4	10	4	9	4	5	9	3	4
Combat weight (kg):	23,496	6,928	15,830	20,000	7,378	9,888	11,249	12,927	4,990	11,830	8,641	7,031
Length overall (cm):	821	446	630	838	570	640	630	640	470	565	383	584
Length of hull (cm):	582	446	630	581	570	569	612	640	470	559	383	455
Width (cm):	320	233	282	279	230	226	244	243	166	244	260	258
Height (cm):	273	215	227	241	240	274	275	212	198	264	213	205
Main gun:	76mm M32	12.7mm M2	152mm M81	Ares 75mm	2 × M73(7.62)	90mm Cockerill			2 × 7.62mm	20mm	6 × M40A1C 106mm	90mm M54
Rounds stowed:	65	1,000	8 mis. 20 con.	60	3,800	39	39				18	29
Secondary armament:	7.62, 12.7mm	7.62mm M60	7.62, 12.7mm	2 × 7.62mm	—	7.62mm	7.62mm	7.62mm	—	7.62mm	12.7mm	7.62mm
Rounds stowed:	5,000/2,175	3,000	3,000/1,000	5,000	—	2,600	2,600				1,000	240
Engine:	AOS1 895–5	Chevy 283	6V53T	Ly. 800	Chry 361	V8–210	440 CID	V–8	Dodge V–8	6V53T	GMC–302	AOI 402-5
Engine type:	petrol	petrol	petrol	turbine	petrol	petrol	petrol	diesel	petrol	diesel	petrol	petrol
Horsepower (hp@rpm):	500@2,800	160@4,600	300@2,800	800	191@4,000	202@3,300	275	250	180@3,600	215@2,800	145@3,400	200@3,000
Power to weight ratio (bhp/tonne):	21.2	23.1	18.9	40	25.8	20.4	24.4	19.3	36.1	18.1	16.7	28.4
Max. road speed (km/hr):	72	58	70	80	100	88	97	97	113	122	48	45
Max. range (km):	160	480	600	325	680	643	483	724	483	1,045	241	225
Ground pressure (kg/cm²):	.75	.36	.49	.63	1.1	1.2	1.3	.94		1.3	.34	.33
Amphibious:	no	yes	yes	no	yes	yes	yes	yes	no	yes	no	no

(3,500 spanning V–150/V–200/V–300)

Abbreviations: Chry, Chrysler; con, conventional; Ly, Lycoming; mis, missiles.

Left: The initial version of the M113 APC with M220 TOW launcher is basically identical to the troop carrier version externally except for the folding mount for the .50 calibre machine-gun. The M220 mount telescopes back into the hull when not in use. Here, a TOW missile is launched from a carrier of the 61st Infantry at Fort Polk in August 1977. This vehicle is finished in the standardized MERDC four-tone temperate pattern. (US Army)

Below: An M113/M220 TOWCAP vehicle of the 3rd Infantry Division supports a Canadian Leopard tank as part of the aggressor forces during the 1977 'Reforger' exercise in Germany. The TOWCAP is a fabric armour tent erected over the TOW mount to protect the crew from overhead shell bursts. It was developed as a temporary expedient prior to the arrival of the M901 ITV in 1979. (US Army)

Right: The M901 Improved TOW Vehicle basically consists of an M113 APC with a twin-tube missile launcher assembly. The elevating mount is designed to allow the vehicle to hide behind hills or buildings with only the launcher and sight assembly exposed to enemy view. (Emerson Electric)

Right, below: The TOW launcher mount on the M901 is designed to fold down to allow the two tubes to be reloaded while the crew remains protected. This is one of the pilot vehicles; the production models have an armour shield added to either side of the roof hatch to provide the loader with side armour protection as well. (Emerson Electric)

were again looking for a small, light anti-armour vehicle.

The M113 TOW. Both the M50 and M56 were very limited in their deployment, and the Army's principal infantry anti-armour vehicle remained the recoilless rifle-armed jeep. By the time of the 1973 Arab-Israeli War, the wire-guided anti-tank missile had finally matured into a lethal and fearsome weapon, and the US Army was just beginning to receive the new MGM–71 TOW. The most common mobile mounting for this weapon, and the earlier recoilless rifle, was the jeep. However, a tracked carrier was desired for mechanized infantry. The obvious solution was to mount the TOW on the M113 APC, and a special retractable M220 mount was developed for this purpose. Externally, the M113 TOW vehicle resembles an ordinary M113 when the M220 mount is retracted. However, internally the vehicle has been entirely reconfigured with provisions for the M220 mount as well as stowage of TOW missile rounds. The main drawback to the M113 TOW was the lack of any armour protection for the crew. In the late 1970s, the Army embarked on a two-phase programme to remedy this situation. In Phase 1, the M113 TOW was provided with a collapsible Kevlar-armour fabric tent on a lightweight tubular frame, which was erected over the rear of the vehicle roof to offer a measure of protection from small-arms fire and overhead artillery bursts. The TOWCAP modification, as it is called, required several minor modifications to the hull roof of the M113, such as provision for fences against which the TOWCAP armour is stowed when not erected. Phase 2 of the programme involved the design of an Improved TOW Vehicle (ITV).

The ITV concept originally stemmed from an ATAC proposal known as the Hardison Concept, which envisaged mounting two TOW launchers on either side of a small turret mounted on the roof of the M113. Personnel at Fort Knox had developed their own approach independently of this venture, mounting two TOW launchers on top of an elevatable 'cherry picker', which would allow the ITV to hide behind natural obstructions, exposing only the launchers to hostile view. In 1975 the Army issued a proposal to industry for the development of the ITV, leading to a third proposal from Emerson Electronics and sponsorship of the two other designs by Chrysler and Northrop. The Emerson version fell somewhere between the other proposals; placing two TOW launchers in an armoured container along with the necessary sighting equipment and mounting it on a rigid elevating trunnion instead of on a telescoping elevatable trunnion as suggested by Fort Knox. The Emerson design was selected for further development in 1976, and the first production models became available in 1979.

The M901 ITV consists of an M113A1 fitted with a new M27 cupola with an armoured launcher assembly attached to it. Supplementary to this major new assembly are several alterations to the hull roof, including the addition of two armoured

planks on either side of the rear hatch which provide full armoured coverage when the rear hatch is opened for reloading the launch tubes. The launcher assembly is only erected when searching for a target or when ready to fire. In transit, it is left folded down on the rear deck. After the first two missiles have been launched, the whole assembly is folded partially backward to enable the loader to replenish the launch tubes. The new launch assembly is adaptable to other vehicles and has already been sold to the Netherlands where it will be mounted on their AIFVs (Advanced Infantry Fighting Vehicles).

Although the M901 was designed primarily for mechanized infantry, it has also been adopted by armoured cavalry as an interim vehicle pending the arrival of the M3 Cavalry Fighting Vehicle. The cavalry had considered adopting the Armoured Cavalry Cannon Vehicle instead, which basically consisted of a 25mm cannon mounted on a remote-control housing over the central cupola, but decided in favour of the ITV rather than adopt yet another vehicle with different logistical requirements into Army service. The Army currently has a requirement for about 2,900 ITVs which will be satisfied mainly by converting existing M113s. The new XM981 Fire Support Team Vehicle (FIST) is a close derivative of the M901. This is an artillery forward observer's vehicle, which uses a modified version of the armoured launcher assembly to house a package of observation gear and a laser designator for illuminating targets for the Copperhead guided artillery round or other semi-active laser homing ordnance. It is also worth noting that, besides the TOW-equipped M113, there is also a vehicle mount for the smaller FGM–77 Dragon anti-tank missile, the M175, which can be fitted to either the M113 or the LVTP–7 in place of the externally mounted machine-gun.

American tank destroyer design and philosophy differs in a number of respects from Soviet practices. Nearly all Soviet tank destroyers are based on armoured cars, while the US Army relies on both unarmoured jeeps and M113s with TOWs. The Soviets do not rely on jeeps as carriers, partly because until the development of the new 9K111 Fagot (AT–4 Spigot), the configuration of their anti-tank missiles was not suitable for use from an unmodified jeep. The US Army has also been a longer and more enthusiastic proponent of the use of helicopters in the tank-destroyer rôle. There were experiments with helicopter-borne SS–11s in the 1960s, but a major turning point came in 1972 when a handful of TOW equipped UH–1s were dispatched to Vietnam where they scored an impressive number of kills against advancing North Vietnamese armour. The Army currently fields TOW equipped AH–1S attack helicopters and is awaiting deployment of the armoured AH–64 helicopter, which will be armed with a 30mm cannon and new Hellfire missiles. In recent years the Soviets have begun deploying their large Mi–24 Hind gunships with AT–6 Spiral anti-tank missiles which have attracted a great deal of attention due to their use in

Afghanistan. No doubt the Soviet use of helicopters in that unhappy country will spur their employment and development by the Soviet armed forces.

One development that will affect the future growth of missile-armed tank destroyers is the controversy over whether these weapons will be effective against the newer generation of tanks protected by the new laminate armours. The dispute first erupted in the US with charges that the TOW is ineffective against the new T–64 and T–72. US Army officials have been reluctant to discuss the question publicly, but from Congressional testimony they seem to indicate that the TOW remains a viable weapon. It would seem that only a small fraction of Soviet armour will be fitted with new types of laminate protection, and a new two-stage effort to improve the TOW's shaped-charge warhead will enable it to defeat improved armour until the TOW replacement becomes available towards the end of the decade.

The whole question of whether missile-armed tank destroyers will remain viable against hordes of improved armour tanks has led some designers to look again at the classic tank destroyer: a light, fast vehicle with thin armour but a big gun. The US Congress has been especially enamoured of the idea of producing large numbers of small, cheap tanks to supplement the expensive M1. One result of this has been the development of the HSTV-L (High Survivability Test Vehicle-Light) as part of the ACVT programme. The HSTV-L bears the unmistakable trademark of AAI which also developed the light T92 during the 1950s. It is a small seventeen-ton tank with a futuristic appearance. What is especially surprising is its novel Ares low-pressure, high-velocity 75mm automatic gun, which fires about sixty rounds per minute. While tank designers have shied away from so small a calibre for many years, new advances in telescoped ammunition and gun technology have led them to re-examine it as a possible alternative for light tank destroyers. Officials are reluctant to disclose the gun's performance, but the gleam in their eyes whenever it is mentioned has led many observers to suspect that a penetration of the frontal armour of a T–62 at 1,000 metres is not out of the question. AAI is currently developing a lighter derivative of the HSTV-L with a two-man crew as a contender for the Marine MPWS (Mobile Protected Weapon System) competition. The Army has supported work on a similar vehicle armed with an automatic 90mm gun.

The Army reorganization under the Division 86 programme envisages a lightly armoured tracked tank destroyer called the MPG (Mobile Protected Gun), which, presumably, would represent the eventual outcome of the HSTV-L and 90mm light gun tank programmes. It is likely that this Army programme, and the Marine MPWS programme will eventually be merged into a single vehicle type, in spite of the fact that the Marine programme stresses light weight to enable the vehicle to be helicopter transportable, while the Army programme stresses the vehicle's anti-armour performance.

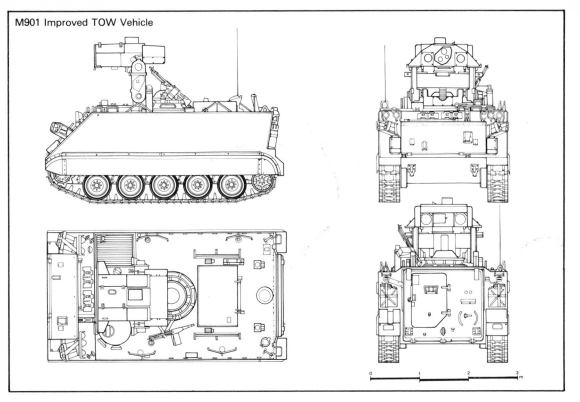

M901 Improved TOW Vehicle

Infantry Combat Vehicles

ARMOURED PERSONNEL CARRIERS

A key ingredient of the 'blitzkrieg' tactics used in the Second World War was the mechanization of the infantry. Ordinary lorries were suitable only up to a point, since they were unarmoured and had poor cross-country performance. The German and American solution to this problem was to develop an armoured lorry which substituted a track suspension for the rear set of wheels, resulting in the ubiquitous half-track. The United States produced a wide series of half-tracks during the war, notably the M2, M3, M5 and M9 series, and used them for everything from troop transport, to self-propelled artillery, to ambulances. The armoured personnel carrier (APC) version was designed for tactical employment as a 'battlefield taxi'; the half-track would offer the troops a measure of protection on the way to their destination, but the infantry would make the actual attack on foot. In fact, half-tracks were frequently used in the attack itself, with the infantry firing over the sides of the vehicle. The M3A1 half-track and its other stable-mates were not the most popular vehicles in US Army service during the Second World War. They became known as 'Purple Heart Boxes' in the North African campaign due to their thin armour. (Purple Heart is the American decoration for wounds suffered in combat.) A more common complaint was their jarring ride on anything but the smoothest road. Nevertheless, they were relatively inexpensive, durable and an important first step in infantry mechanization.

The Army began developing more suitable infantry vehicles towards the end of the war. Using the chassis of the M18 tank destroyer and M24 light tank, the M39 and M44 were developed. Unlike the M3A1 half-track, the M44 was fully armoured and fully tracked. It offered both better cross-country mobility and better protection for the infantry since it had roof armour. In common with the M3A1, it could also be used in a variety of other rôles, such as artillery tractor or battlefield ambulance for stretcher cases. The M44 was not ready before the conclusion of the war, but was used in small numbers during the Korean War. An improved model, the M44E1, was built which dispensed with the side doors in favour of new roof hatches and also incorporated new automotive improvements. Besides serving with the Army, a number of M44s were used by the Air Force as tactical air control (TACP) vehicles. The M44 was the first of a new generation of APCs featuring full armour protection and a fully tracked suspension, but its large size rendered it somewhat unpractical for many rôles and it was not entirely successful.

The M75. The M44 could carry twenty-three men but the Army realized that a smaller APC might be more desirable and in 1945 it began work on a twelve-man carrier based on the chassis of the T43 cargo tractor. Although appreciably smaller than the M44, the new carrier was not much lighter, but was better designed for the entry and exit of its troops. In recognition of its primary rôle, its designation was changed from armoured utility vehicle to armoured infantry vehicle and it was accepted for Army use in 1952 as the M75. The M75 was arranged in a fashion that would become standard on American APCs for the next three decades. The engine was housed in the front right-hand corner of the vehicle for easy access, and the driver sat aside to the left. The commander's position was in the centre of the vehicle, behind the engine. He had a small circular cupola with vision blocks on the roof, and controlled an externally mounted .50 calibre M2 heavy machine-gun. Behind him in the rear compartment were bench seats for eleven infantrymen and their equipment. The M75 shared automotive and suspension components with the M41 light tank. A total of 1,729 M75s were completed before production ceased in 1954. The M75 was produced by two different firms, and there were a number of detail differences between the two production batches. Some M75s were used during the Korean War, mainly as armoured ambulances.

The M59. The main drawback to the M75 was its height and high cost. Its air cooling grilles were exposed on the sides and the front hull glacis plate, and the two rear doors, while an improvement over the M44, were awkward to exit from. As a low-cost solution, ATAC developed a stretched version of the M50 Ontos, called the T56, ten-man personnel carrier-fighter, and also developed a troop carrier version of the M56 Scorpion. Neither was very satisfactory. Independently, FMC, which up to this point had concentrated mainly on developing Marine amphibious tractors, offered the Army a new APC which was smaller and lighter than the M75 and was also fully amphibious. The Army was intrigued by the offer, and even though the M75 was only beginning to enter production, funded further development. This vehicle eventually materialized as the M59. The M59's main advantage was that it only cost about a quarter of the M75 yet was amphibious, simpler to produce and had a more convenient layout for troop exit. It had a simple, boxy hull design with all-engine cooling grilles on the roof. Its internal layout was similar to the M75, but at the rear it had a single, large power-operated hatch for troop exit. The vehicle was buoyant in water; when swimming, a front bow plane was folded down to prevent water washing over the roof. The vehicle was propelled forward by the action of its tracks. The power plant consisted of two commercially available engines and transmissions identical to those used in the two-and-a-half-ton truck, one powering each track.

International Harvester, the designer of the M75, offered the Army a cut-down and cheaper version of the M75, the T73. However, in competitions with the M59, the T73 was not found to be as suitable. As a result, the Army took the unusual step of ordering the M59 into production to supplement the M75, even before M75 production had ceased. It was finally decided to produce a sufficient number of M59s to replace all M75s in service, most of which were then handed over to the Belgian Army. The M59 was supposed to be fielded with a fully protected machine-gun for the commander, but there were delays in developing this feature and on the first contract batch of 2,385 vehicles the

Left, below: The principal armoured troop carrier of the US Army during the Second World War was the M3A1 half-track, which was withdrawn from US service after the Korean War but still remains in use throughout the world. It served with distinction in Israeli hands during the Middle East wars. Many of the Israeli vehicles, such as this one, incorporated various improvements, including diesel engines.

Top: The M75 was the first major armoured troop carrier designed and manufactured for the US Army after the Second World War. It could accommodate thirteen troops, but was very expensive and not amphibious. Although it was quickly replaced by the M59, it continues on in service with the Belgian Army. (US Army)

Middle: There were several attempts to develop cheap, tracked troop carriers, including this short-lived attempt using the chassis of an M56 Scorpion SPAT. (US Army)

Below: Two M59s participate in winter manoeuvres during Exercise 'Caribou Creek' in Alaska, 1959. The vehicle with the machine-gun cupola is from the later production batch, while the rear vehicle is from the initial batch, which had an exposed pintle mount for the machine-gun. (US Army)

machine-gun was externally mounted. The new cupola, the M13, became available in 1956 and the final production batch, designated M59A1 Armoured Infantry Vehicle, were produced with this feature. In all, there were slightly more than 4,000 M59 and M59A1s produced, as well as a 4.2in mortar version, the M84.

The M59 was not without its problems in service use. The dual engine arrangement was frequently troublesome, and the M59 proved to be under-powered and not fast enough to keep up with M48 Patton tanks on manoeuvres. Its amphibious qualities were not entirely adequate and, since the freeboard was so slight, the vehicle could be swamped in moderately choppy conditions. Nevertheless, the M59 was a substantial improve-ment over previous types and was available at a low enough cost and in large enough numbers to further infantry mechanization. The problems with the M59 led in 1955 to the decision to design a new carrier vehicle that could be used as the basis for a variety of armoured support vehicles. A contract was issued to FMC to develop this carrier in two forms: one using conventional steel armour, and the other using new aluminium armour technology.

The M113. The new carrier was called the Airborne, Armoured, Multi-Purpose Vehicle Family, with the aluminium armoured personnel carrier designated T113 and the steel prototype called the T117. There were twenty-six different body configurations under consideration for the family, including an ambulance, cargo carrier, mortar carrier, anti-tank guided missile launcher, flame-thrower, counter mortar radar vehicle, forward area light anti-aircraft weapons carrier and an artillery multiple rocket launcher version. The aluminium armoured version proved to offer several advantages over the steel version. Although the aluminium armour was about as heavy as the steel armour to enable a comparable level of ballistic protection, it was considerably thicker. This thickness contributed to high rigidity in the hull without the use of reinforcement required in the steel version, so that, overall, the aluminium version weighed less than the steel prototype. As a result, in 1959 the T113 was accepted for Army service as the M113 APC and ordered into production. So began the career of one of the most successful post-war armoured vehicles.

The M113 closely resembled the M59, though there were several external changes, most notably its lower height and the transfer of the commander's cupola back towards the centre of the vehicle. The driver is positioned in the front left-hand corner of the vehicle and operates the M113 by means of a conventional set of steering levers. To his immediate right is the compartment containing the engine and transmission. The engine is easily accessible through a large hinged panel at the front of the M113. The squad commander plus ten infantrymen ride in the rear of the vehicle, with a back-to-back jump seat under the cupola and bench seats on either side. Equipment is stowed over either mudguard, with the vehicle radios carried on the left wall. Exit from the vehicle is through the rear ramp, but there is a large hatch on the roof that allows a portion of the infantry squad to ride partially outside the vehicle or to exit over the side. The M113 is fully amphibious and, like the M59, depends on the track for propulsion. It has a maximum speed of about 5.5km/hr in the water. It is light enough to be easily air transported. Its armament consists of a single .50 calibre M2 heavy machine-gun on an exposed external pintle.

The first modification programme undertaken was the substitution of a diesel 6V53 engine for the older 75M petrol engine. This was meant to increase the operational range of the M113, and was part of the Army's plan to switch to diesels for their fuel economy advantages, beginning with the intro-duction of the M60 tank into the armoured divisions in 1960. The first diesel-powered M113s, designated M113A1, were produced in September 1966 and have subsequently become the standard production model. There are no significant external differences between the M113 and the M113A1.

The M113 served as the basis for a host of other vehicles, both proposed and actually manufactured.

Left, top: The first combat use of the M113 APC came in Vietnam. This ARVN M113 was fitted with an FMC M24A2 twin machine-gun turret in place of the usual exposed .50 calibre M2 machine-gun. (James Loop)

Left, middle: During the ARVN's initial combat actions with the M113, it became painfully obvious that the machine-gunners on top of the vehicle were very exposed to enemy fire. As a result, various improvized shields (shown here) were manufactured. Later in the war, kits became available from Okinawa and, subsequently, from the United States. These M113s served with the 2/7th Cavalry, 1st ARVN Division in I Corps, 1970. (US Army)

Left, below: Troops of the 2/47th Infantry, 9th Infantry Division take cover behind an M113 armed with a 75mm recoilless rifle, after recovering a wounded soldier during fighting south of the 'Y' bridge near Saigon, 11 May 1968. (US Army)

Top: A column of M113 ACAVs of Troop A, 3/4th Cavalry, 25th Infantry Division, return to Landing Zone 'Hampton' after a reconnaissance mission in Vietnam on 3 August 1969. The rolls of chicken wire were used as protection against RPG – 7 rockets when the vehicles were at rest at night. (US Army)

Below: This overhead view of an M113 of the 11th Armored Cavalry before its departure for Vietnam in 1966 clearly shows the standardized ACAV armoured shield kit used on APCs in Vietnam. (US Army)

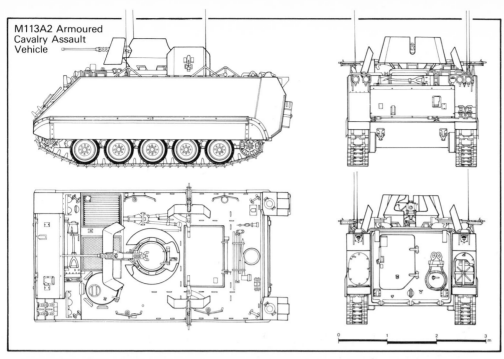

M113A2 Armoured
Cavalry Assault
Vehicle

Top: There have been several fire support versions of the M113 developed, including this turreted type with a Cockerill 90mm gun and a Cadillac Gage turret and fire control system. (Cadillac Gage)
Below: The M113 is among the most successful armoured vehicles of all time and one of the most widely produced. In addition to its military rôle, it is also used by UN forces to monitor peace agreements. This UN M113 is patrolling the area between Israel and Syria near Mount Hermon in December 1975. (United Nations)
Right, top: An M113 and M60A1 of the 4/73rd Armor take a breather during exercises near Grafenwohr in the summer of 1976. The four-colour, Seventh Army camouflage scheme has not been painted over the rubber dust skirts of the M113. (Brian Gibbs)
Right, below: An M113 with M220 TOW launcher of the 2nd Brigade, 8th Mechanized Division, on a road near Romrod, Germany, during the 1976 'Reforger' exercise in the autumn of 1976. It is finished in a four-colour Seventh Army scheme and carries the temporary insignia of an aggressor unit for use during the wargames. (US Army)

Among the most important of these was the M548 family of unarmoured cargo carriers. These use the chassis and automotive components of the M113, but the hull configuration above the line of the mudguard differs considerably. The M577 Light Command Post is essentially a standard M113 with the rear compartment raised to allow staff officers to stand up to read maps and carry out their duties. At the forward portion of this compartment, a gasoline-driven generator is carried to provide electricity for lights and radios. The M577 also carries a large tent that can be erected at the back of the vehicle to provide more space for the command centre. The M577A1 version is a diesel-powered model comparable to the M113A1. The M577 is used by headquarter units, artillery fire control units and other command and control elements, and serves as the basis for a number of electronic and radio command posts. The basic M577 can be readily converted into a field ambulance and there are field modification kits to enable litters to be carried. The most important combat derivatives of the M113 are the M106 4.2in mortar carrier, the M125 81mm mortar carrier and the M167 Vulcan air defence vehicle.

The M113 first made its reputation during the Vietnam War. It was supplied initially to ARVN in 1962, and was quickly dubbed the 'Green Dragon'. The M113 never received a universally accepted nickname in US Army service, and is usually called simply an 'APC', 'PC' or 'Poppa Charlie', from its official designation 'Armoured Personnel Carrier'. The initial use of M113s by the ARVN according to US tactical doctrine caused the US Army to rethink its mechanized infantry tactics. It was quickly found that rather than have the infantry disembark and attack an objective on foot, it was better to attempt to overrun an objective with the infantry fighting from the top of the carrier so long as the objective was not heavily protected by anti-tank weapons. The main drawback of the M113 to these new tactics was that it had not been designed to provide the infantry on it with a real measure of protection, and the crewman operating the front .50 calibre machine-gun was especially vulnerable to hostile fire. As a result, the Vietnamese, in co-operation with American advisers, began developing light armour shields from scrapped half-tracks, and more suitable armament packages. The usual arrangement was to build a thin armour parapet around the .50 calibre, protecting the operator from all sides but the top, and add two M60 7.62mm machine-guns behind shields on either side of the rear roof hatch. Subsequently, a stop-gap kit was manufactured in Okinawa and eventually FMC manufactured standardized kits. In the US Army, M113s fitted with the factory-manufactured kit were usually called ACAVs (Armoured Cavalry Assault Vehicles). There were two basic kits available, one consisting only of the .50 calibre cupola armour and another with this armour and the two M60 shields. These remarks hardly begin to encompass the wide range of armament and modifications carried out by the US Army in Vietnam. Other arrangements included 7.62mm Gatling guns, 40mm automatic grenade launchers, various types of recoilless rifles, airfield matting used as improvized stand-off armour to protect against RPG – 7 rocket launchers, chain link wire stand-off armour and many others. No US M113s in Europe or Korea used the kits due to their cost.

The success of the M113 in Vietnam was due to its excellent mobility, durability and design. It was reliable, could withstand a surprising amount of punishment considering its light armour, and its large rear compartment made it very versatile in different tactical rôles. Its low cost meant that it was available in large numbers. The diesel-powered versions were preferred since they were not as prone to catastrophic internal fires due to mine or rocket damage. Mines and RPG – 7s were the most serious threat, and many drivers liberally padded the floor with sand bags and improvized armour under their seats. Many troops preferred to ride outside the APC where the view was better and there was less risk from mines; some M113s of the 25th Infantry Division had the driver's controls extended outside

the hull so that the driver could steer while sitting outside.

In view of the changing tactics brought about by the war, there were several attempts to develop suitable modifications for the M113. The Infantry School at Fort Benning developed the XM765, which added firing ports to the side of the vehicle and moved the bench seats back-to-back along the centre. Vehicles with firing ports as well as other modifications, such as bar armour, were experimentally tested in Vietnam, but few of these features were incorporated in the production models.

The success of the M113 in Vietnam coupled with its very low unit cost led many nations to adopt it as their standard troop carrier. Over forty-one countries use the M113, and total production of the series has exceeded 75,000 vehicles with manufacture still continuing. Besides FMC's main manufacturing facility in the United States, the M113 has also been produced overseas by OTO-Melara in Italy. The largest user outside the United States Army is the Israeli Zahal, which fields in excess of 5,000 M113s and used them in the 1973 Arab-Israeli War. The M113 is the most widely produced American tracked armoured vehicle of all time and, with the exception of the British Bren Carrier, and the Soviet T – 34 and T – 54/55 tanks, more have been produced than any other armoured vehicle. There have been dozens, if not hundreds, of modifications of M113s in foreign service. Many of these are armament changes with the substitution of power turrets for the usual .50 calibre cupola. These have ranged from the installation of small Cadillac Gage twin .30 calibre machine-gun turrets to the installation of 76mm and 90mm gun turrets. For example, the Australian Army modified some of their M113s into fire support vehicles by adding the turret from the Saladin armoured car, and later improved this by the substitution of a turret from the Scorpion light tank. Several firms offer turrets specially tailored for use on the M113, and some of these are shown in the photographs here. The most radical conversion of the M113 was the joint FMC/Rheinmetall Fire Support Combat Vehicle which added a casemate mounted 105mm howitzer. There has been a constant series of technical improvements to the basic M113 besides these many armament

Left, top: An M113 serving as an OPFOR vehicle during the 1978 'Reforger' manoeuvres hides in a stand of pine trees near Fort Polk, Louisiana. The red-circled black star is the insignia of OPFOR units, which simulate enemy formations during training. Note that the infantryman in the rear is wearing a plastic pseudo-Soviet helmet. OPFOR units also use various types of captured Soviet tanks and armoured vehicles and M551 Sheridans. (US Army)
Left, below: The replacement for the M113 finally emerged in 1979 as the M2 Bradley infantry fighting vehicle, and its twin, the M3 Devers cavalry fighting vehicle. Both vehicles are nearly identical externally, though this particular vehicle is configured as the M2. The rectangular armoured container on the turret side folds upward to expose two TOW launchers. On the hull side below the TOW launchers can be seen two of the firing ports for the crew. (FMC)
Top: One of the standard variants of the M113 family is the M577 command vehicle. Two M577s of the 2nd Armored Division in place during manoeuvres at Fort Hood in 1975; they are shown here with their spacious tent sections erected over the rear. (Brian Gibbs)
Middle: An interior view of an M577 command vehicle, showing the map tables and seating arrangements as well as the radio equipment. (Brian Gibbs)
Below: An unarmoured version of the M113, the M548 cargo carrier, is widely used by many armies to carry supplies, especially for self-propelled artillery units. This M548, towing a water trailer, served with the 11th Armored Cavalry in Vietnam in 1968. (James Loop)

additions. In 1978, the first M113A2s were produced. These featured an improved cooling system, strengthened suspension and a dual air source heater that allows employment of a collective CBR system. Many M113A1s will be converted eventually to M113A2 standards. FMC also developed external fuel tanks for use on the M113A2 conversion, though at the last moment the US Army decided against adopting this feature. However, the external fuel tanks have been purchased by some export clients, notably Israel. The M113A3, which was type classified in 1980, features a new transmission and a more powerful turbo-charged 6V53T engine. This version also has strengthened torsion bar suspension and other features to offer better cross-country performance. These vehicles will begin to enter service in about 1983. FMC independently developed a number of other M113 variants primarily for the export market. The first of these, the M113 Command and Reconnaissance, or M113½, was a cut-down scout version adopted by Canada, Belgium and the Netherlands. The Advanced Infantry Fighting Vehicle (AIFV) was another private venture by FMC incorporating an improved rear hull shape with external firing ports. Several different armament options were offered with this vehicle and it has been sold in quantity to the Netherlands, both with a gun turret and with an ITV TOW launcher. A similar vehicle, the IAFV (Infantry Armoured Fighting Vehicle), was developed by OTO-Melara for use by the Italian Army. One of the more recent M113 variants is the M113A1–S, which is a stretched version with an added set of road wheels to allow more cargo or troops to be carried.

The M2 and M3. In spite of the great success of the M113, it is essentially configured for the rôle of 'battlefield taxi'. Its main duty is to transport its infantry squad safely to their objective, and disembark them to attack the objective on foot. While modifications such as the ACAV kit allowed it to be employed as an assault vehicle in Vietnam, against a well-equipped opponent like the Warsaw Pact forces this would not be practical. The other drawback to the M113 is that it was designed to keep pace with the M60, and is too slow to follow newer designs such as the ill-fated MBT–70 or the new M1. Owing to these tactical shortcomings, in 1963 the Army began searching for a replacement, called the MICV–65 (Mechanized Infantry Combat Vehicle). The principal requirements for the MICV were provisions to allow the infantry to fire their weapons from within the protective armour of the vehicle, sufficient power to keep up with the MBT–70 in cross-country travel, and armour sufficient to defeat 14.5mm fire. FMC developed a number of possible candidates for the competition, including the Product Improved M113, a more mature version called the XM765, which would later become the AIFV, and the XM723. However, the contract went to PACCAR, which offered its XM701, an infantry assault vehicle based on the M107/M110 self-propelled gun.

The XM701 proved to be a disappointment, as it exceeded the specified weight and did not fully live up to the requirements. Funding for the programme dried up due to the high costs of other armoured vehicle programmes, such as the MBT–70, but more importantly due to the escalating costs of the Vietnamese War. The MICV programme languished until 1972. The conclusion of the war in Vietnam made it possible to consider once again the need for a new type of infantry vehicle, but the real spur to its development was the public appearance of the Soviet BMP infantry combat vehicle in November 1967. The BMP embodied all the features the US Army had sought in the MICV–65. It was well armed, very fast and agile, and allowed its infantry squad to fight from within the protective shell of the vehicle. Other European armies were also adopting similarly sophisticated vehicles, notably the German Marder. In 1972, FMC was awarded a contract to proceed with its XM723 as the new MICV. The venture progressed, though not without difficulty, until 1975, when a major development changed the orientation of the programme. The Army cancelled the cavalry's ARSV programme, feeling that it

Left, top: Although various attempts by FMC to interest the US Army in a product improved version of the M113 came to naught, a derivative of these efforts, the AIFV, is being used by the Dutch Army, who call it the YPR–765. It features a redesigned hull with firing ports for the troops, and a 25mm cannon-armed turret. (Emerson Electric)

Left, middle: The first attempt to replace the M113 was the XM701 MICV–65. This was developed by PACCAR and used automotive components from the M107/M110 self-propelled guns. It exceeded Army weight requirements and was dropped from further consideration, though the chassis was used later as a test bed for the GLAAD anti-aircraft system trials. (US Army)

Left, below: The MICV programme was resuscitated after the Vietnam War. FMC then developed the XM723, which resembled their AIFV export vehicle but was more heavily armoured and better engined. The decision in 1976 to merge the MICV programme with the cavalry's attempt to design a new scout vehicle led to the redesign of the M723 to accommodate a two-man turret. The result of this venture eventually materialized as the XM2/XM3 IFV/CFV. (US Army)

Right: This close-up of the M2 turret shows the TOW launchers elevated and ready to fire. The M2 is armed with TOW and a 25mm Bushmaster cannon, which can effectively deal with nearly any light armoured vehicle. There are four smoke launchers on either side of the turret, plus various racks for ammunition and personal stowage. (FMC)

Below: This starboard side view of the M2 shows clearly that the design is not symmetric; while the port side firing ports are in the centre of the vehicle, on this side they are to the rear. The M2 uses a collapsible screen similar to that on the M551 Sheridan to provide enough freeboard for the vehicle to swim across rivers and lakes. (FMC)

created a needless proliferation of different tactical vehicles. The cavalry was instructed to join with the infantry in developing the MICV into a vehicle acceptable to both branches, and in August 1976 a MICV Task Force was formed purely for this purpose.

The XM723 used a 20mm gun mounted in a single crewman turret. The cavalry wanted a two-man turret with a fully stabilized gun and some anti-tank capability to match the BMP. As a result, FMC worked in conjunction with Hughes to develop a new turret armed with a 25mm Bushmaster automatic cannon firing depleted uranium kinetic-energy penetrator rounds as well as more conventional forms of ammunition. The turret armament was to be fully stabilized and a coaxial M240 machine-gun incorporated. To provide long-range anti-tank capability, the designers took a cue from the Soviets and incorporated a twin TOW missile launcher to deal with armour too heavy for the 25mm gun. The resulting vehicle with the TBAT–II turret (TOW-Bushmaster Armoured Turret/two-man) was called the IFV/CFV (Infantry Fighting Vehicle/Cavalry Fighting Vehicle). There was some curious criticism of the programme on the grounds that by mounting an effective anti-armour system the IFV would suddenly become a prime target for the attention of Soviet tank guns, therefore the new IFV should be armoured to protect itself from such a heavy calibre threat. This would have meant a complete redesign, since the IFV was designed only to withstand 23mm fire, and would have resulted in a 50-ton infantry carrier. Fortunately, this suggestion was ignored. The IFV and CFV came under more prolonged criticism because of their high unit cost compared to the M113, but cost studies found that other solutions were not as effective. For example, although the AIFV was less costly than the IFV, in order to improve its armour, firepower and mobility sufficiently to satisfy the IFV requirements, it would be no cheaper than the IFV/CFV. What many critics failed to appreciate was that the IFV did not aim

simply at developing a better-armed M113 with firing ports, but rather a vehicle which offered a major improvement in mobility and armoured protection as well. While this debate continued, the new IFV/CFV vehicles were completing their trials with considerable success, leading to type classification in 1980 as the M2 IFV and M3 CFV.

The M2 and M3 are basically identical vehicles externally, and differ internally in regards to stowage and other features. Initially, the M3 was to carry a motorcycle inside for use in independent scouting, but this was ruled out due to the hazard an unprotected petrol tank would pose to the vehicle. The main differences between the M2 and M3 are that the cavalry version does not use the firing ports, has less floor armour, fewer crewmen and therefore has greater stowage of ammunition and TOW rounds. The M2 has a configuration similar to the M113. As has become standard on American infantry vehicles, the driver is stationed to the left, with the engine and transmission, behind bulwarks, filling the forward right-hand corner of the vehicle. The TBAT – II turret is in the centre of the vehicle. It is largely self-contained due to the use of a turret basket. Behind this and to either side is the crew compartment. To the left of the turret are two riflemen who use the left-hand side firing ports, two riflemen back-to-back along the right rear side using the right firing ports, and two other riflemen in the rear centre and rear left corner firing through the two ports in the back ramp. The M3 has only two soldiers in the rear compartment.

The main armament of the M2/M3 is the M242 Bushmaster Chain Gun, with a coaxial M240 7.62mm machine-gun. The standard 25mm rounds for the Chain Gun are an anti-tank hyper-velocity round with depleted uranium penetrator and a high-explosive incendiary round for use against other targets. Two ammunition boxes are used to allow a choice of ammunition type, and the weapon is fully stabilized along three axes through the use of an inertial gyro stabilizer. All fire controls are duplicated so that either the vehicle commander or the gunner

can control and fire the weapons. The TOW launchers are folded against the right side of the turret in an armoured container. The armoured container is folded up for launching, exposing the missiles. The missiles are guided using the same sight as the main gun, the ISU (Integrated Sight Unit), which incorporates both a day sight and a thermal imaging night sight. The MGM – 71 TOW guidance is similar to that used on other TOW systems: semi-automatic wire guidance in which the gunner keeps the target in the cross-hairs of his sight while the missile is fed automatically electronic course corrections over the wire until impact. The 25mm gun is capable of defeating most armoured targets short of main battle tanks, and is believed to have a penetration of about 75mm of steel at 0° at 1,000m, though the exact performance is still classified.

The M2/M3 is armoured to withstand 23mm fire from its frontal arcs, and uses a variety of steel, steel-aluminium laminates and aluminium armour to achieve this while retaining light vehicle weight overall. Even though the M2/M3 is some seven tons lighter than the German Marder, it is more heavily armoured. The M2/M3 is also fully amphibious. A swimming skirt, similar to that used on the M551 or FV432, is stowed along the upper edge of the hull, and is unfolded to provide the vehicle with enough freeboard to float. As in the case of the M113, it is propelled through the water by its tracks. Exit from the vehicle is by a large rear ramp, and there is also a large roof hatch through which the TOW launchers are reloaded. On the M2, the crew is armed with the 5.56mm M231 Firing Port Weapon. This is basically an M16 rifle with a folding metal stock and an adaptor which allows it to be attached to the vehicle's ball socket firing mounts. Sighting is through individual periscopes.

The Army has requirements for over 6,000 M2 IFVs and about 3,300 M3 CFVs. The first completed production machines are expected in 1981. The M2s will be used to replace M113s in those armoured divisions equipped with M1 Abrams, while the

Left, below: This rear view of the M2 shows the main exit ramp. There is also a roof hatch, which is used to reload the TOW launcher after the first two rounds have been expended. In this view, the TOW launcher is erect. The suspension of the M2, though resembling that of the M113, was in fact derived from the LVTP – 7 AmTrac. (FMC)
Below: The definitive replacement for the M551 Sheridan and M114 in cavalry service is the M3 Devers cavalry fighting vehicle. It is a derivative of the M2 Bradley infantry fighting vehicle with a smaller crew and modifications to the internal stowage. (FMC)

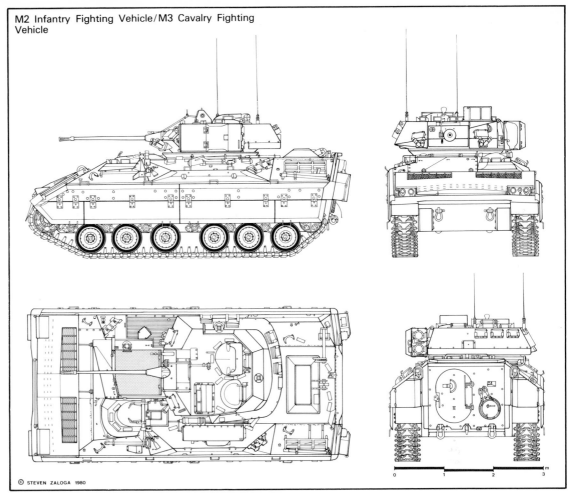

M2 Infantry Fighting Vehicle/M3 Cavalry Fighting Vehicle

© STEVEN ZALOGA 1980

M113s will continue to serve in units with M60s, with the Reserve and National Guard and in supporting tasks such as command posts, electronic support vehicles and the like. The M3 will be deployed to armoured cavalry units to replace M901s, M113s and M60s that were introduced as temporary expedients following the premature phase-out of the M114 and M551. In comparison to the BMP, the M2/M3 has advantages in nearly every category: it is more heavily armoured, more mobile and better armed. Its stabilized 25mm gun has a much better chance of a quick kill against a BMP than vice versa, due to the eccentricities of the 73mm low-pressure gun used on the BMP, and the TOW is a more accurate and lethal weapon than the 9M14M Malyutka (AT–3 Sagger) missile used on the BMP. The actual accuracy of Soviet riflemen from the BMP's cramped interior is considerably less than the accuracy from the IFV due to the better suspension of the M2 over rough terrain. One key feature missing from the IFV/CFV is CBR protection, but this will be installed in the form of a collective protection system rather than an over-pressure system as favoured by the Soviets. The names 'Bradley' and 'Devers' have been proposed for the M2 and M3 after the two famous World War Two generals.

AMPHIBIOUS TROOP CARRIERS
One type of armoured vehicle pioneered by the US Marines and virtually unseen in other armies is the LVT (Landing Vehicle Tracked), popularly called AmTracs (from amphibious tractors). These were originally designed to assist Marine assaults in the bloody amphibious landings of the Pacific campaign, and received their baptism of fire at Tarawa in 1943. During the war, these vehicles slowly metamorphozed from unarmoured tractors to well-armed and armoured assault vehicles. There were two principal varieties, an open-topped troop carrier, such as the LVT–3 and LVT–4, and a gun-armed support vehicle, such as the LVT(A)1 and LVT(A)4. The major AmTrac type used after the war was a modernized version of the LVT–3, the LVT–3C, which had an armoured cover added to the roof and a machine-gun cupola at the bow. The LVT–3C was used extensively during the Korean War, and is certainly best known for its rôle in the Inchon landing.
The LVTP–5. The outbreak of the Korean War prompted the Marine Corps to reassess its AmTrac needs, and a crash programme was undertaken to develop a replacement for the LVT–3C. Two proposals were offered: from Ingersoll Steel and Disc a massive design which could be produced as a troop carrier for thirty-seven men or as a howitzer support vehicle; and a proposal from FMC which was in essence an amphibious version of their M59 APC. The Ingersoll design was chosen due to its better handling qualities in water and surf, and its larger cargo capacity. A contract was issued and the first production vehicles were completed in the summer of 1951. The two initial versions were the LVTP–5, a personnel and cargo version, and the LVTH–6, a turreted support version mounting a 105mm howitzer. This vehicle was one of the most massive, armoured tracked vehicles ever adopted for service use in the US. Several specialized versions of the LVTP–5 were subsequently developed, including the LVTCR–1, a command version with additional radios; the LVTR–1, a recovery vehicle with jib boom; and the LVTE–1, an engineer vehicle with a massive plough blade, line detonation charge, and other modifications for demolition work.
The LVTR–5 was designed to carry a crew of three, plus thirty-four seated combat troops; as many as forty-five troops could be carried at a pinch. The P–5 had its engine at the rear, and the troop compartment forward. Exit was through a large bow door. The P–5 was propelled through the water by track grousers. Production of the series continued through 1957. The final production batch had several improvements, including a one-speed final drive, removal of rear hull rudders and installation of box schnorkels over the roof ventilators. These

Top: The first of the post-war AmTracs was the gargantuan LVTP–5, which had a large exit ramp at the front of the vehicle as well as hatches on the roof. This LVTP–5A1 of the 4th Marines is bringing supplies and reinforcements forward during a sweep against North Vietnamese troops near Cua Viet, May 1968 (USMC)
Middle: In addition to the troop carrier version of the LVT–5 series, there was also a howitzer support version, the LVTH–6A1, armed with a 105mm howitzer. This vehicle was supporting an advance by the 1st Marine Division in Vietnam at the end of January, 1968. Its ammunition can be seen stacked in the packing tubes in the lower left corner. (USMC)
Below: The engineer version of the LVT–5 series, the LVTE–5A1, was popularly called 'Potato Digger' by Marines in Vietnam due to its enormous V-shaped plough. On the roof was a launcher for minefield breaching charges. This particular vehicle is supporting the 2/5th Marines during Operation 'New Castle' in Vietnam, March 1967. (USMC)
Right: The standard version of the LVT–7 family is the LVTP–7 personnel carrier. Troop exit is via a rear ramp, though a model with roof hatches is available, as can be seen here. The basic vehicle armament is a machine-gun cupola, but a special mount for the Dragon anti-tank missile has also been developed. (FMC)

vehicles were redesignated LVTP–5A1 and LVTH–6A1. There were a number of other experimental versions of the P–5 family, but none was accepted for quantity production.

The LVTH–5A1 and its related derivatives were used extensively in Vietnam. They proved very suitable for beach assault, but their enormous size made them less appropriate for operations beyond the beach area. The P–5 was also very thinly armoured, fairly expensive and complicated to maintain, and the location of the fuel between the floor and belly armour caused brew-ups when mines were run over. Some of these shortcomings had been anticipated, since the P–5 had been designed with an emphasis on performance in the water and immediate beach area and had never been intended as an across-the-beach assault vehicle. In 1963 it was decided to begin development of a smaller, less costly vehicle with better overall performance. A contract was issued to FMC and the first prototypes were ready in 1965. Production followed and the first of these vehicles, designated LVTP–7, entered Marine service in 1971.

The LVTP–7. The P–7 had a different design criteria to the earlier P–5: it carried a troop complement of only twenty-five as opposed to thirty-four in the P–5, and had a reduced cargo capacity. Nevertheless, it was faster on land and

water, had better fuel economy and range, was better armed and armoured and weighed some eighteen tons less. The configuration of the two types differ considerably. The engine compartment on the P–7 is in the bow, which serves also to protect the troop compartment from frontal hits during assault. The troop compartment has a large exit ramp at the rear of the vehicle, whereas the P–5 has a bow ramp. The weapon cupola on the P–7 is armed with a .50 calibre machine-gun, and can be fitted with an external M–175 Dragon mount. A powered turret armed with an M139 20mm cannon had been developed for the P–7, but this was rejected due to problems with the gun. The P–7 is designed to carry about five tons of cargo, and doubles as a ship-to-shore cargo carrier once the troops have disembarked. The main advantage of the P–7 over amphibious troop carriers used by marine units of the Warsaw Pact, such as the BTR–50, is that the P–7 can survive and operate in ten-foot high surf and suffer total immersion with a full cargo compartment without sinking.

A family of related support vehicles was built on the P–7 chassis, as was the case with earlier AmTracs. The LVTC–7 is a command version, closely resembling the P–7, but without the machine-gun cupola and with additional radio and command gear. The LVTR–7 is a recovery version

with a power-operated boom. The LVTs are organized into assault amphibian battalions with a headquarters company and four assault amphibian companies. The headquarters company has fifteen P–7s, three C–7s and one R–7. The assault amphibian companies have four platoons, each with ten P–7s, and a headquarters platoon with one P–7, three C–7s and three R–7s.

The P–7 is rapidly approaching its service life expectancy with a replacement vehicle nearly a decade away from production. As a result, a SLEP (Service Life Extension Programme) is underway to rebuild key components and introduce some modifications. The new LVTP–7A1 will incorporate a new engine and transmission, the installation of an automatic fire suppression system, a new secure voice communication unit, passive night sights for the driver, mountings for a PLRS navigation unit, ventilation improvements, a new fuel tank, and an M257 smoke grenade launcher developed from a British system. There will be similar modifications in other members of the LVT–7 family. The modification programme will be accompanied by a new production programme. The new production LVTP–7A1 has several small external differences from the improved LVTP–7, such as smaller, square headlight enclosures and mounts for the antenna at the rear of the troop compartment. The

Far left: This view of an LVTP – 7 of the 2nd Amphibian Tractor Battalion at Camp Lejeune, North Carolina, clearly shows the large, rear loading ramp, and also the circular nozzle for the water jet propulsion system used to power the AmTrac when in the sea. (USMC)

Below: The LVT – 7 series was somewhat more modest in size than the LVT – 5 series, but was faster and better armoured. This vehicle is an LVTC – 7 command vehicle of the 2nd Marine Division, shown here during NATO exercises in the Mediterranean in February 1977. It has additional communication equipment, but, unlike the P – 7 personnel version, does not have the usual machine-gun cupola on the starboard side. (USMC)

Left: A scene reminiscent of a John Wayne film: reservists from the 3/25th Marines storm ashore at Coronado, California, in best Marine tradition, with a wave of LVTP – 7 AmTracs immediately behind them. (USMC)

new production is expected to amount to 288 P−7A1, 27 C−7A1 and 12 R−7A1.

Design of a replacement for the LVT−7 family was delayed by budget constraints and some dispute as to the configuration the vehicle would take. Many Marine officers were concerned that the design criteria for past LVTs had placed excessive emphasis on the water performance of the AmTracs, resulting in vehicles with very poor combat performance out of water. Consideration was also paid to the possibility that an air-cushion suspension might not be a more effective system than tracks. These alternatives were studied under the LVA (Landing Vehicle Assault) programme which was abandoned in 1979. In 1980, a follow-on programme was begun with a request for proposals from industry regarding a replacement for the LVT−7. The new vehicle, currently called LVT−X, will be smaller and better armoured than the LVT−7, and the personnel version is likely to be armed with a 25mm Bushmaster cannon similar to that used on the Army's IFV/CFV. The Marines have also dropped the cargo handling requirements for the new LVT−X which had inevitably led in the past to rather massive vehicles. Design criteria call for higher land speed as well. The Marines hope to have the new vehicle in service by 1990.

INFANTRY COMBAT VEHICLES

Designation:	M44	M75	M59	M113	M113A1	M113A2 (external fuel)	M2	M3	LVTP-5A1	LVTP-7
Production:		1,729	4,000		70,000 +		6,000[1]	3,300[1]	1,123	1,579
Crew and troops:	27	13	13	13	13	13	9	5	37	24
Combat weight (kg):	23,632	18,824	18,960	10,387	11,156	11,737	22,045	21,802	38,193	22,838
Length (cm):	660	518	561	487	487	530	645	645	904	794
Width (cm):	307	274	314	269	269	269	126	126	355	327
Height (cm):	282	274	276	252	252	252	117	117	304	326
Main armament:	12.7mm M2	12.7mm M2	12.7mm M2	12.7mm M2	12.7mm M2	12.7mm M2	25mm M242 + 2	TOW	7.62mm	12.7mm
Rounds stowed:	550	1,800	1,800	2,000	2,000	2,000	900/7	1,500/12	2,000	1,000
Secondary armament:	7.62mm	—	—	—	—	—	7.62mm M240	7.62mm M240	—	—
Rounds stowed:	420	—	—	—	—	—	2,340	4,540	—	—
Engine:	R975D4	AO 895-4	2 × GMC 302	Chrysler 75M	6V53	6V53	VTA-903T	VTA-903T	AV 1790-1	8V53T
Engine type:	petrol	petrol	petrol	petrol	diesel	diesel	diesel	diesel	petrol	diesel
Horsepower (bhp@rpm):	475@ 2,400	375@ 2,800	2 × 146@ 3,600	194@ 4,000	158	156	506	506	810	400
Power to weight ratio (bhp/tonne):	13.5	18.0	14.0	18.0	19	18	20.6	20.8	21.2	17.5
Max. road speed (km/hr):	51	69	51	68	68	68	66	66	48	64
Max. range (km):	290	185	193	321	483	483	483	483	305	482
Ground pressure (kg/cm²):	.59	.57	.50	.51	.55	.58	.53	.52	.65	.57

Notes: [1] Anticipated production in initial contract batch.

Left: The LVTP−7A1 has many internal improvements over the P−7, but externally is fairly similar. The only major points of identification are the square headlight covers, the raised cupola behind the driver's cupola, and the radio masts mounted on the rear. (FMC)

Right, top: The M37 self-propelled 105mm howitzer entered production at the end of the Second World War and saw service in Korea. It was based on the M24 light tank and resembled its predecessor, the M7, in general configuration. Here, M37s of the 58th Field Artillery Battalion fire at Chinese positions across the Imjin River on 12 April 1951. (US Army)

Right, below: The M43 self-propelled 8in howitzer was based on a modified Sherman tank chassis. It remained in service throughout the Korean War, after which it was gradually replaced by the M55. This vehicle, 'Killer', of the 780th Field Artillery Battalion, moves into firing position in the Punchbowl area in Korea in 1953.

LVTP-7A1 amphibious tractor

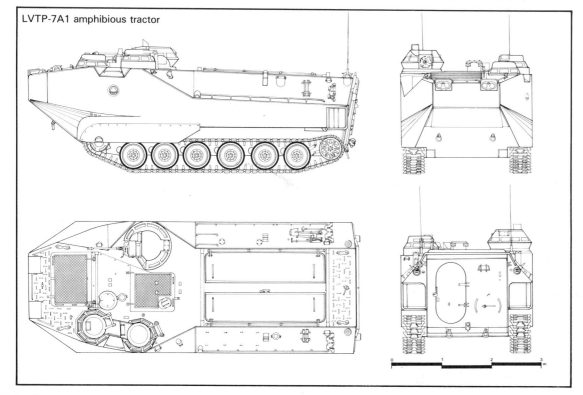

Mechanized Artillery

The US Army was bereft of self-propelled artillery at the start of the Second World War, with only a handful of improvized half-track mounted guns in service. Nevertheless, by the war's conclusion, a larger portion of its artillery had been mechanized than in any other army. The vast majority of self-propelled guns were based on tank chassis, usually medium tanks. The most widely produced type was the M7 Priest self-propelled 105mm howitzer. This remained in service in dwindling numbers after the war, mainly with Reserve and National Guard units, though it was widely employed by many other armies in front line service. It was a durable, robust vehicle, if only because the chassis was not grossly overloaded as was the common fate of many improvized self-propelled artillery pieces during the war. A small number of 155mm M12s were also built on an M3 Lee chassis, but none of these remained in service after the war. A modified Sherman chassis was used to produce the M40 155mm self-propelled gun and the M43 self-propelled 8in howitzer, which were virtually identical apart from the gun tube and ammunition stowage racks. These were straightforward designs, and remained in service throughout the Korean War. They were not widely exported like their smaller stable-mate, the M7.

Two other self-propelled artillery pieces completed their trials and entered production at the end of the Second World War, but too late for combat. The M24 Chaffee light tank was designed with an eye towards developing a series of interrelated armoured vehicles, and two of these were the M37 self-propelled 105mm howitzer and the M41 self-propelled 155mm howitzer, sometimes called the Gorilla. The M37 mimicked the design of the M7 Priest, complete with a 'pulpit' on the right side. On the other hand, the M41 resembled the M40, with its weapon perched on the very end of the vehicle and a large rear spade to absorb the recoil of the howitzer. Both the M37 and M41 saw extensive combat action in Korea. While most of the self-propelled artillery used by the US Army during the Second World War was thinly armoured and open-topped, armoured units did employ tanks that had been reconfigured to use short-barrelled howitzers to provide fire support. The two most significant of these were the M4 (105mm howitzer), which resembled an ordinary M4 Sherman but with a thick, stubby barrel, and the M8 75mm Howitzer Motor Carriage, which was an M5A1 Stuart light tank with a new open-topped turret and 75mm howitzer. The M8 was phased out after the war, though the M4 howitzer tank served on through the Korean War. This type of self-propelled artillery fell from favour after the Second World War.

SELF-PROPELLED GUNS

The excellent service provided by self-propelled artillery during the war led the Army to convene a special War Department Equipment Board in 1946 to assess the needs for more modern equipment and to begin design work. The main drawbacks of the wartime designs were their limited armour cover over the weapon and their restricted traverse. They were difficult to load, and their fire controls were usually little different from the types used on wheeled artillery. It was decided to build two basic families of self-propelled artillery: a light type, comprised of the T98 105mm self-propelled howitzer and the T99 155mm self-propelled howitzer, which would replace the M37 and M41; and the T97 155mm self-propelled gun and T107 8in self-propelled howitzer, which would replace the M40 and M43. These families would be built using the light tank components from the forthcoming M41 Walker Bulldog light tank and M48 medium tank. For these new vehicles, two forms of fire controls were developed: the 'ultimate type', which used full-powered elevation; and a simpler 'alternate system', which was mechanically less complicated. To surmount the traverse problem with the older wartime types, it was decided to mount the weapons in a lightly armoured turret.

The M44 and M52. The prototypes for both the T98 and T99 were ready in 1950, though there were complications brought about by engineering changes in the M41 light tank. During trials it was evident that the 'ultimate' fire control system was unworkable, and the T98 was fitted with the simpler type for production as the M52 self-propelled 105mm howitzer. In common with many of the tracked vehicles rushed into production during the course of the Korean War, the M52 was plagued by major difficulties that had not been ironed-out during trials. These required modifications that

delayed issue until 1955. The T99 closely resembled the T98 in its original form, and was put into production. Unfortunately, the decision proved premature, as the alternate fire control system proved totally unsatisfactory and there were many other problems with the basic design. About 250 vehicles had been built before production was halted. A modified derivative, the T194, was developed which corrected these problems but required extensive modification to the fighting compartment. The roof armour was removed and a barbette mount rather than a turret was used for gun traverse which limited the weapon to a small frontal arc. The T194 was accepted for production as the M44 self-propelled 155mm howitzer, and the unsatisfactory T99E1s were rebuilt to these standards.

The M53 and M55. The T97 and T108 were designed to employ an identical mount, so that the only significant difference between both vehicles was the gun tube, ammunition stowage racks and minor stowage items. The first prototypes were delivered for trials in 1952 and the first production models followed less than four months later. There were a considerable number of problems, as had been the case with the smaller T98 and T99, which led to a modification programme in the summer of 1955. The vehicles were not suitable for issue to the troops until 1956. In the meantime, the Army decided against the use of the 155mm gun version and ordered all of its vehicles to be issued as the 8in howitzer version. As a result, when issued to the troops, the Army used only the M55 self-propelled 8in howitzer, while the Marines used the M53 self-propelled 155mm gun. There were plans to field a 175mm gun version in place of the M53 in Army service to provide better long-range firepower, but this effort was postponed owing to the difficulties with the M53 and M55 and delays in developing the new gun. The M55 never saw combat service in the hands of US troops, though the M53 was used by the Marines in Vietnam until replaced by the M109. The M52, M44, M53 and M55 arrived in Army service at a time of a major rethink about American strategy in Europe and the rest of the world. There was increasing concern that the US should be able to rapidly reinforce its divisions overseas more promptly than had been the case in Korea. Air transport improvements offered the best hope of accomplishing this, yet, in spite of substantial advances in aircraft design, armoured vehicles presented a real problem due to their bulk and weight. Little could be done with tanks, since weight reduction implies unacceptable armour reduction. However, in the case of armoured personnel carriers and self-propelled guns, significant weight reductions were possible through the use of aluminium armour, as well as reductions

Left, top: The M40 was essentially similar to the M43 but used a 155mm gun tube. It served with distinction in the Second World War and remained in use throughout the 1950s. This M40 served with the 18th Field Artillery Battalion as part of the aggressor forces during Exercise 'Cordon Bleu' in Germany in October 1955. Like the gun on which it was based, the M40 was usually called the 'Long Tom' by the troops. (US Army)

Left, middle: The M44 self-propelled 155mm howitzer was initially designed with a fully enclosed turret, but problems with the first production batches led to a rebuilding programme in which the gun compartment was redesigned without overhead armour. These M44s served as part of the 534th Field Artillery Battalion at Fort Sill in 1955 and carry the Armoured Corps emblem prominently on their hull sides. (US Army)

Left, below: An M52 of 78th Field Artillery Battalion, 2nd Armored Division, crossing a Class 60 bridge during Operation 'Big Lift' near Babenhausen, Germany, in October 1953. The M52, like the M44, was based on the M41 light tank as part of an effort to develop a family of armoured tracked vehicles sharing common components. (US Army)

Above: The M53 and M55 were similar vehicles essentially but used different gun tubes. The M53 self-propelled 155mm gun remained in Marine service through the early years of the Vietnam War and was eventually replaced by the M109. This M53 served with the 1st Marine Division in Vietnam in January 1968. (USMC)

Right: There were a number of attempts in the late 1950s to develop an extremely light self-propelled howitzer for use by airborne troops, culminating in the XM104. However, it was not adopted for service use. (US Army)

Above: The M108 self-propelled 105mm howitzer was the last weapon in its class to be adopted by the US Army. Its career was short-lived; by the time of its introduction into service in the mid-1960s, it was felt that the related M109 self-propelled 155mm howitzer was more suitable. Subsequently, no self-propelled 105mm howitzer have been designed for Army use. These camouflaged M108s served with B Company, 40th Armor, at Fort Sill in July 1966. (US Army)
Left: The M109 self-propelled 155mm howitzer first saw combat in Vietnam in 1966. This rear view of an M109 in Vietnam shows the turret traversed around to the 4 o'clock position, with the recoil spades still folded up. Wooden chocks have been put under the front of the road wheels to help absorb the blast. This vehicle served with the 23rd Artillery Group near Phu Loi in 1968. (James Loop)
Right: The M109A1's most distinctive feature is its very long barrel. Two M109A1s of the Israeli Army are seen here in the Sinai, with an M577 command post in the background. (Israeli Defence Force)

in bulk by more patient design efforts than the hasty and slap-dash attempts of the Korean War period.

The M108 and M109. The programmes that germinated between 1952 and 1956 envisaged developing two chassis in the light and heavy categories, as had the 1946 programme. The first conference, held in 1952, outlined the broad guidelines of the effort, and was followed in 1954 by a study which laid out the fire control requirements for the new vehicles. In 1956 and 1957, the technical requirements for the new vehicles were summarized and contracts issued. The light category was to be represented by a self-propelled 110mm and 156mm howitzer sharing common vehicles, and the heavy category was to encompass three heavy artillery pieces on the same chassis and mount. In the light category, it was recognized that the choice of new calibres for the howitzers would entail logistical problems with existing towed artillery, and the more conventional calibres of 105mm and 155mm were substituted shortly after wooden mock-ups had been produced. The two vehicles in the light category were the T195 self-propelled 105mm howitzer and the T196 155mm self-propelled howitzer. The principal difference between the vehicles was the addition of spades at the rear of the T196 to absorb the heavier recoil of the larger howitzer, as well as necessary improvements in the power elevation system for the weapon. The T195 prototype was ready in 1959 and underwent tests before the more complex T196 became available. Serious modifications to the suspension were needed; also, during the trials the Army, in keeping with the new move pioneered by the M60 tank programme, decided to switch to a diesel power plant with its better fuel economy. Production was suspended in order to work out carefully all the problems that had been discovered in the

suspension and final drive assembly; this decision contrasts markedly with the treatment accorded their predecessors, which had been rushed to the production stage. Production for both vehicles was finally authorized after strenuous testing in 1961, with the first production models coming off the lines in 1962 as the M108 105mm light self-propelled howitzer and the M109 155mm medium self-propelled howitzer. Production of the M108 lasted only a year. Although the vehicle lived-up to its requirement, the Army decided that the 105mm howitzer was too small a weapon to justify the cost of a large tracked chassis and the 155mm howitzer was more effective. Use of the M108 by Active Army divisions was short-lived, and much of the production was provided to allies such as Belgium who use it to this day.

The M109 on the other hand is still in production nearly twenty years after its initial batch left the assembly lines. It has proved to be a robust and dependable vehicle, and its careful design has allowed important modifications to enhance the performance of the vehicle. The M109 uses a six-man crew, consisting of a driver, commander, gunner and three ammunition crewmen. The large turret is carried at the rear of the vehicle, and there is ample access through rear and side doors. The vehicle uses aluminium armour and is air transportable. It is not amphibious without preparation, but a kit is available which provides air bags for attachment to the sides of the vehicle. When firing, the rear spades are lowered to absorb the howitzer's recoil. The usual rate of fire is a round a minute, though it can burst-fire at three rounds per minute for a short duration. It can also fire a nuclear round.

The M109 first saw combat during the Vietnam War. The first major deployments came in 1966 and included small numbers of M108s. The M109 had

been designed to fight a mobile war against fast-moving, mechanized forces. Vietnam was very different, and the M109 fought as often as not from prepared static positions. Nevertheless, its sound construction and mobility permitted a worthwhile adaptation to its unexpected rôle. The M109 saw its real test in the 1973 Arab-Israeli War. The M109 had been used by Israel along the Suez in 1970, but it was the crises of 1973 that proved its true mettle.

Operations in Vietnam highlighted the need for longer range performance from the M109's howitzer. Work began on both improved ammunition, notably RAP (rocket assisted projectiles), as well as basic engineering modifications consisting of a new longer barrel, improved elevation and strengthened turret traverse, and reinforcement of the suspension to enable it to withstand the heavier recoil of the new howitzer. The PIP kit (Product Improvement Programme) was ready in 1972, and the first converted M109A1s entered service use in 1973. In addition to the modification of existing M109s, new vehicles were also manufactured with these features plus other small changes. These new vehicles were designated M109A1B. The M109A1B remained in production until 1979, at which point the improved M109A2 was introduced. The M109A2 closely resembles the M109A1 as most of the modifications — such as a new M178 gun mount, simplified hydraulics, and new safety features — are internal. Some external indicators of the conversion are the new ballistic sight cover on the forward left-hand corner of the turret roof, and the increased size of the rear turret bustle to accommodate more ammunition. As in the case of the M109/M109A1 programme, a PIP kit was also made available to convert the M109A1 to meet these standards. These modified vehicles are designated M109A3.

Below: The new M109A2 closely resembles the M109A1 but incorporates many internal improvements. Externally it is distinguishable from the earlier model by the square ballistic shield over the gun sight on the forward left-hand corner of the turret roof, and by a lengthened rear turret bustle, which is not evident in this view. (BMY)
Right, top: A desert-camouflaged LVTP – 7 takes part in Operation 'Palm Tree' with the 2nd Marine

Division in California, March 1976. This camouflage pattern is derived from the patterns and colours developed by MERDC for the US Army. (USMC)
Right, below: This view of Bravo Battery, 3rd Infantry Division, emplaced during the 1977 'Reforger' exercise near Weinreid, Germany, clearly shows the extreme elevation angle possible with the M109A1. The circled green triangle is the temporary insignia of the aggressor forces during wargames. (US Army)

M109A2 155mm self-propelled howitzer

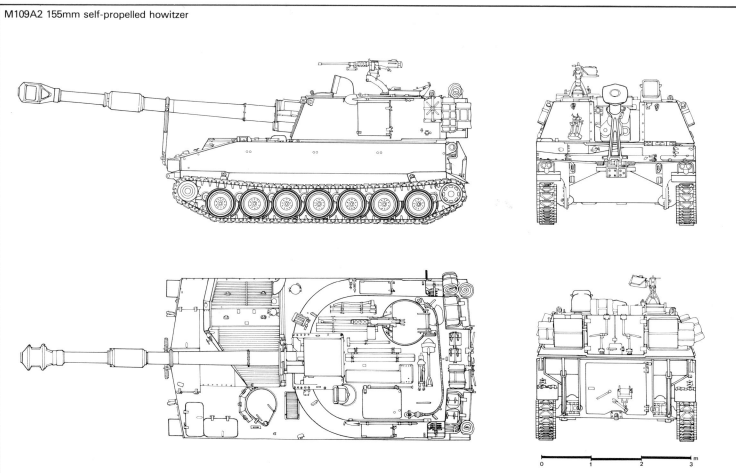

The M107 and M110. The heavy counterparts to the M108/M109 family were the T235 self-propelled 175mm gun, the T236 self-propelled 203mm howitzer and the T245 self-propelled 155mm gun. This family of vehicles took the commonality programme one step further. Not only did the vehicles share a common chassis, but the gun tubes were readily interchangeable. A central aim of the programme was to drastically reduce the weight of the vehicle in order to make it air transportable. To accomplish this it was necessary to abandon the turret armour and develop a unique suspension lockout system that allowed the fairly light chassis to absorb enormous recoil forces. The prototypes underwent initial testing in 1958, and the trials proceeded far more smoothly than those with the M108/M109. As in the case of their smaller siblings, the heavy family had diesel engines substituted for petrol engines in 1960. It was felt that the 155mm gun version did not offer any significant advantages over the other two weapons and, as a result, when production was authorized in 1961, only the two larger calibre weapons were chosen for quantity production. These were designated the M107 self-propelled 175mm gun and the M110 self-propelled 8in howitzer. Both types became operational in 1963. It is worth noting that a light armoured recovery vehicle was based on the same chassis, the M578, but has not proved as popular as the artillery versions due to its small lifting capacity. The M107 and M110 both suffered from minor teething problems during their initial deployment, particularly the hydraulic system, the loader and the rear spades, but these problems were corrected without much ado. Consideration has been given spasmodically to providing the firing platform crew with a tent of Kevlar fabric armour, but this has not been standardized.

The M107 was employed as a corps support weapon, and could fire a 66kg projectile about thirty-seven kilometres at a rate of one a minute. The enormous pressures built up by full charges in such a long gun tube created a great deal of tube wear, and the barrel life expectancy was only about 1,200 rounds at full charge. The M107 was deployed with both the Army and Marines. The M110 could fire a 42kg projectile about seventeen kilometres and had a longer barrel life. Both the M107 and M110 had crews of thirteen men, consisting of a driver, commander, three gunners and the remainder assigned to ammunition duty. The vehicle was not designed to carry the full crew, though its large size enables it to do so at a pinch. Ordinarily, the crew travels in accompanying M548 cargo carriers, which are also employed to carry the vehicle's ammunition. The M107 was organized into battalions with twelve guns each and assigned at corps level, while the M110 was assigned at divisional level with a battery of four in each infantry division and a battalion of twelve in each armoured or mechanized division.

The M107 and M110 were deployed in Vietnam and performed yeoman service in the support rôle. It was difficult sometimes to classify the vehicles as one model or another, as in some situations individual chassis would be fitted with a 175mm tube one day and have an 8-inch tube substituted the next for other missions. The extremely long range of the M107 was particularly appreciated for interdiction missions, and co-ordination of fire was arranged with the help of Forward Air Control aircraft, as well as more conventional means. As in the case of the M108s and M109s serving in Vietnam, the M107s and M110s proved very adaptable to their tasks, even though they had not been designed for an anti-guerrilla war. After the Vietnam War, the most extensive combat use of the M107 took place with the Israeli Army. The M107s were heavily involved in the fire fights along the Suez in 1970, where their long range proved a distinct advantage. The great value that Zahal placed on these weapons can be garnered from the fact that, during the 1973 war, among the first weapons rushed over the Suez Canal were M107s, to be used to wipe out the surface-to-air missile sites that had been so severely restricting the ability of the Israeli Air Force to carry out close-support missions. The M107 and M110 were both extensively exported

Left, top: Dusters in Vietnam were usually attached to artillery units for use in the perimeter defence rôle. This M42A1 of B Battery, 4/60th Artillery, is overlooking Landing Zone 'Uplift' near Qui Nhon in October 1967. (US Army)
Left, below: The winner of the Army's contract for a self-propelled air-defence gun system, the twin 40mm Bofors XM988 DIVAD.
Top: An M109A1 of the 2/41st Field Artillery, 3rd Infantry Division, moves up during summer exercises in Germany, 1976. (Brian Gibbs)
Middle: One aspect of the HELBAT artillery studies was the examination of methods to increase the rate of fire of self-propelled artillery units. BMY and AAI each developed tracked reload vehicles, such as this M109 Ammunition Delivery System by BMY, which feeds rounds to the howitzer by means of a conveyer belt. (BMY)
Below: The M107 and M110 were widely used in Vietnam to provide fire support. These vehicles were designed with readily changeable barrels, and it was not uncommon in some field artillery units to have a single vehicle configured one day as an M110 self-propelled 8in howitzer and the next day as an M107 self-propelled 175mm gun. This M110, ironically dubbed 'Sounds of Silence' after the popular Simon and Garfunkel tune, was firing in support of C Company, 1/11th Infantry, 5th Infantry Division, near the Demilitarized Zone in October 1970. (US Army)

Above: An emplaced M110 self-propelled howitzer of Battery B, 8/6th Artillery, at Fort Riley, Kansas, in August 1971. (US Army)
Left: All M107 and M110 self-propelled howitzer chassis in US Army service are being reconfigured into the improved M110A2, which features a new longer barrel and muzzle brake. This view shows a brand new M110A2 with its tube retracted in the travelling position. (BMY)
Right, top: This view of an M107 self-propelled 175mm gun of 2/28th Field Artillery, Battery A, clearly shows the long slender barrel that characterized this weapon. This gun was taking part in the 'Reforger V' exercise near Ansbach, Germany, in October 1973. Some M107s were fitted with canvas tents to provide a measure of protection for the gun crew in bad weather. There were also trials with Kevlar fabric armour tents to protect the crews from overhead shell bursts. (US Army)

and are the primary heavy self-propelled guns of the British Royal Artillery.

In 1969, the US Army took steps to improve the M110's long-range performance by the development of a new rocket-assisted projectile and the design of a new longer barrel. This version was type classified in 1976 as the M110A1 and entered service the following year. The new modifications extended the range of the M110A1's howitzer comparable to that of the M107, and so it was decided to convert the M107 battalions to M110s. In the meantime, a muzzle brake for the new M110A1 had been developed which allowed the howitzer to fire heavier propellant charges. The M110A1s were manufactured to readily accept the new feature; vehicles fitted with the muzzle brake are designated M110A2. The M110A2 can fire conventional projectiles approximately thirty-five kilometres and rocket-assisted projectiles, such as the M650, approximately forty kilometres at a rate of about one every two minutes. There were about 300 M107s in Army service in 1979 and a further 400 with the Marines, but these will be phased-out by the addition of the new 8-inch tube and added to the 450 M110s in service (as of 1979).

The United States Army has not been particularly anxious to develop replacements for either the M109 or M110 families, as both vehicles have proved to be very satisfactory in service and constant improvements in ammunition and barrel technology have extended their useful life. Moreover, other aspects of artillery technology have not really kept pace with the advances in self-propelled guns, such as fire control, target acquisition and counter battery detection, ammunition handling and site surveying. Greater attention is now being paid to these areas.

One promising area that is being enthusiastically explored is precision guided munitions. The first of these, the Copperhead round, is currently being developed for use with the M109A2. The Copperhead is a new cannon-launched laser guided round designed to knock out tanks and other precision targets with a very high probability of a first-round kill. The Copperhead uses a semi-active laser guidance system. To function, a forward observer team, such as a team in the new XM981 FIST vehicle mentioned earlier, spots a target and radios to the artillery crew to fire a Copperhead round into the general vicinity of the target. The Copperhead is fired like a conventional round, though after its departure from the tube, small wings fold out to stabilize the round and provide guidance. Once the round is fired, the forward observer illuminates the target tank with a laser designator. The Copperhead's sensor acquires the invisible coded laser pulse that has been reflected off the tank, and steers the round to the target. While mobile targets such as tanks would require on average about 200 rounds of conventional artillery ammunition to knock them out, with a Copperhead round this can be accomplished with one or two rounds. The main drawback is that the laser designator is not entirely effective if there is thick cloud or smoke cover, though newer CO_2 lasers to alleviate this problem are being developed. A round similar to Copperhead is being developed for the Marine's M110A2s. There are other types of guided rounds currently under development, such as a radio frequency homing round for the M110A2 which is designed to home-in on the beams of hostile radars. Probably the most ambitious of these new ammunition types is the AIFS (Advanced Infra-red Seeker) being developed for the M110A2. The AIFS

is a ramjet-assisted anti-armour round with a small, sensitive imaging infra-red seeker in the nose. This is connected to a sophisticated programmed microprocessor that can interpret the images picked up by the seeker and guide the round to a tank by its shape, heat pattern and the infra-red discrepancy between the tank and the ground. A similar round is also contemplated using a millimetre wave radar instead of an infra-red seeker. The principal advantage of the AIFS over the Copperhead is that it does not require the co-operation of a laser designator and also is operable virtually in all weather.

Aside from these ingenious new artillery rounds, other more prosaic improvements are being contemplated for the M109 and M110. The establishment of the Navstar Global Positioning System, a satellite-based navigation system that broadcasts to ground-based sets precise information on their exact location, will revolutionize artillery surveying both due to its speed and accuracy. It will allow self-propelled guns to become rapidly emplaced without time-consuming surveying, and allow them to avoid counter battery bombardment. Another improvement is the development of automated ammunition handling equipment, like the new FAASV XM992 (Forward Area Artillery Supply Vehicle) being considered. This consists of M108 chassis taken out of mothballs with their turrets replaced by an ammunition stowage compartment and conveyor belt assembly. This vehicle can rapidly feed fuzed ammunition into an M109A2 under full cover of armour. There are also numerous other examples of fire control and target acquisition improvements being considered under the HELBAT programme which space does not permit coverage of here.

M110A2 8in self-propelled howitzer

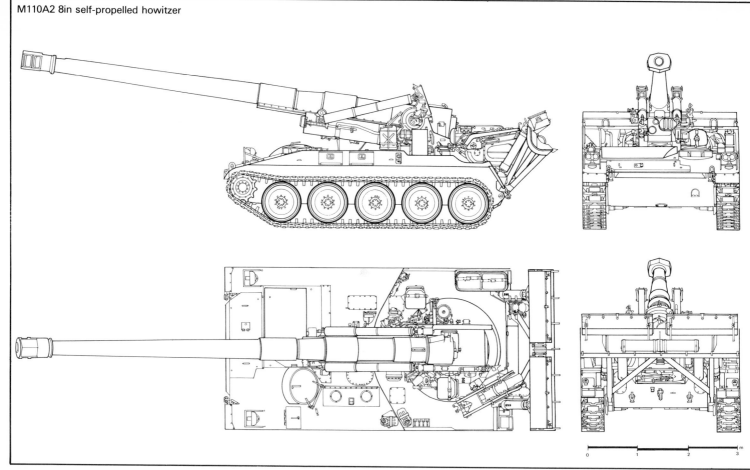

Left: Several derivatives of the M107/M110 self-propelled guns were developed, including the XM701 MICV – 65 infantry vehicle, but the only one built in sizeable numbers was the M578 light armoured recovery vehicle. This vehicle is used to carry out repairs on lighter armoured vehicles, such as the M113, or light repairs on tanks, such as engine replacement. (BMY)

Right, top: The XM993 MLRS is the first multiple rocket launcher system to have progressed so far in development for the US Army since the Second World War. There were attempts to mount an array of Little John rockets on the M113, but this plan fell through. The MLRS uses the FVS tracked chassis – developed by FMC from the M2/M3 series – and will probably serve as the basis for other tracked utility vehicles such as forward armoured supply carriers. The cab is fully armoured and can be sealed during rocket firing. The current Vought rockets are unguided, but guided payloads are under development. (Vought)

Right, below: This view of the XM993 MLRS shows the rocket array folded into travelling order. The entire system has been designed for use with a three-man crew. (Vought)

MISSILE LAUNCHERS

The numerous requirements of modern self-propelled weapons has prompted the Army to begin study of the desirable characteristics of such a system under the DSWS (Divisional Support Weapon System) programme. Both PACCAR and FMC have received contracts to begin these studies, and under consideration are vehicles which would incorporate automatic loading systems or systems more heavily automated than those used in current vehicles. Another possible configuration that will be studied is the casemated gun, where the main weapon is not provided with full traverse but rather the entire vehicle is moved to aim the gun. Such a configuration has been criticized in the past, since it obligates the vehicle to keep its motor running in order to permit aiming compensation, though such a system would provide the gun with a few degrees of traverse to permit fine adjustments.

The United States Army is badly outnumbered by the Soviet Army in the total number of artillery tubes in service, but the US Army has always had a larger portion of its weapons on self-propelled mounts. Only recently have the Soviets begun deploying comparable weapons such as the new SAU – 122 self-propelled 122mm howitzer, the SAU – 152 self-propelled 152mm howitzer and the even newer self-propelled 203mm howitzer and 240mm mortar which have not yet been displayed publicly. One area in which the Soviets have always shown a great deal of interest is multiple tube rocket launchers, or Katyushas. These artillery weapons are not as accurate as conventional tubed artillery, but are fairly cheap to manufacture and are useful for heavy area-saturation fire. The US Army used these types during the Second World War, both in the form of tank-mounted and lorry-mounted multiple tubed arrays, but they became unfashionable in the post-war years. Consideration had been given to building a version of the M113 APC with a Little John multiple rocket launcher, but this fell through.

The Multiple Launcher Rocket System (MLRS).
In 1976, the Army issued contracts to initiate the GSRS programme (General Support Rocket System), subsequently renamed the MLRS (Multiple Launcher Rocket System). It was decided to develop the weapon competitively, with Vought and Boeing each offering their own conception. To speed up the programme, both prototypes used an FVS tracked vehicle, an armoured utility vehicle based on the M2/M3 IFV/CFV and designed by FMC. Vought was chosen after firing tests in 1979

and 1980. The MLRS consists of the FMC XM993 tracked carrier with an armoured launcher assembly on a traversable platform at the rear. The cab of the vehicle houses the three-man crew and the vehicle is provided with armoured shutters to cover the windshield on firing, and an air filtration system. The rocket launcher assembly contains twelve unguided .9in (227mm) rockets armed with an M42 submunition dispenser warhead. These rockets can be fired in pairs or rippled fired, and have a range in excess of thirty kilometres. Each rocket contains over 600 submunitions, and scatters them over an area about 100 metres long. The launch assembly has a built-in derrick, which permits rapid reloading of palletized rounds by a single crewman. The launcher can be reloaded by a single six-pack, or both sides can be reloaded simultaneously. Although the MLRS was designed primarily as an anti-personnel saturation weapon, new warheads are under development for other rôles, including scatterable anti-tank mines, guided anti-tank bomblets using imaging infra-red or millimetre wave seekers, and general cargo loads such as smoke, illumination, unattended ground sensors, electronic jamming devices, fuel-air explosives and chemical munitions.

XM993 Multiple Launcher Rocket System

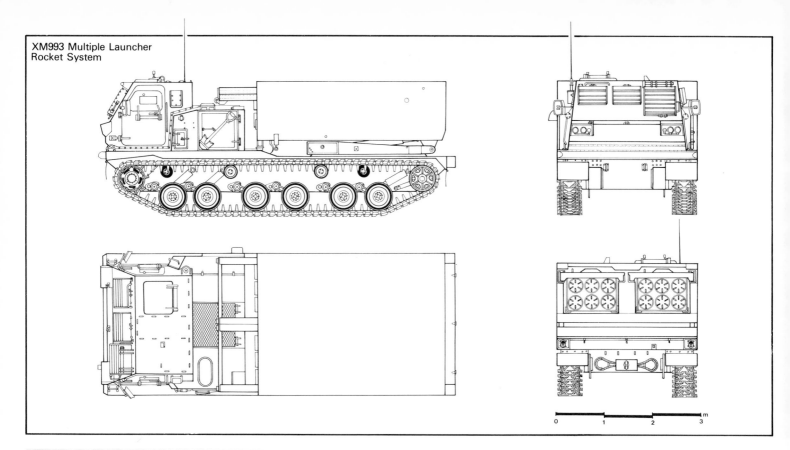

Middle: The XM993 MLRS has been designed to be reloaded by one crewman. The rocket rounds are contained in six-round pallets that can be loaded separately or in pairs, as shown here. These expended rounds are being jettisoned, with a pair of loaded pallets ready behind the vehicle. (Vought)

Below: The M106 self-propelled 4.2in mortar carrier closely resembles the M113 armoured personnel carrier on which it is based, but is readily distinguishable at a distance by the large mortar bridge and base plate stowed on the left side of the hull. A large circular port with folding doors was added to the roof of the hull rear. The major modifications were internal. This M106 from the 11th Armored Cavalry was photographed in Vietnam by one of the authors, September 1968. (James Loop)

Right, top: The M84 self-propelled 4.2in mortar carrier was a derivative of the M59 armoured personnel carrier, with the rear area modified to permit firing of the weapon. This rear view shows an M84 in firing mode at the ranges at Camp Roberts, California, in the spring of 1958. (US Army)

SELF-PROPELLED MORTARS

The M84. Besides the use of tracked carriers for artillery, the US Army has also used tracked vehicles to carry heavy infantry weapons such as mortars. During the Second World War, the most common type was a half-track mounted 81mm mortar. In 1945, the Army began to investigate possible carriers for the 4.2in (107mm) mortar, and settled on a modified M37 self-propelled howitzer with its armament removed. This proved to be a satisfactory arrangement with adequate room for the crew and ammunition, but as the M37 was to be replaced, adoption might have caused spares' problems. In common with many other immediate post-war projects, the T38 4.2in self-propelled mortar faded from view. In 1950, with the Korean War in progress, interest in a tracked mortar carrier was revived. In view of its rôle as a heavy infantry weapons carrier for use with mechanized infantry units, the use of an armoured infantry carrier seemed the most sensible. Three models were proposed using the M75 APC as a transporter: the T62 81mm carrier, the T63 105mm carrier and the T64 4.2in carrier. All three vehicles were fairly similar with sufficient armour in the rear of the vehicle removed to allow the mortar crews to service the weapon efficiently. By the time the prototypes had been tested, it was evident that the new M59 APC was about to enter service and, in view of the cost of the M75, it was felt prudent to await the new carrier. In any event, the M59 made a more suitable platform and only required modification of the upper roof panels to provide an adequate field of fire and allow the crew to move about. These were type classified in 1954 as the M84 4.2in mortar carrier; production began in 1956.

The M125 and M106. The M84 suffered the same shortcomings as its parent vehicle, the M59, and as a result was produced in small numbers. In 1956 it was decided to begin studies on a similar conversion to the new M113 APC. The new mortar carrier was to be designed to accommodate either the 81mm or the 107mm mortar, with appropriate alterations for stowage difference. The initial prototypes used the petrol engine, but prior to the decision to start production, the diesel version became available and it was decided to modify the prototype vehicles to accommodate the diesel. Petrol-powered carriers were accepted for limited production in 1961 as the M125 81mm mortar carrier and the M106 107mm

mortar carrier. The first diesel-powered versions, the M125A1 and M106A1, were produced in 1965.

The basic alterations to the M113 chassis are the same as on the M125 and M106. The rear area of the roof has been reconfigured, with a large circular port covered by two large doors that fold outwards towards the side. The mortars are mounted on a large circular platform on the rear floor bed, and ammunition stowage is provided in either sponson. Externally, the M125 is very difficult to distinguish from an ordinary M113 APC, unless the rear roof panel is evident. In contrast, the M106 has a large mortar bridge and base plate stowed externally on the left side of the hull; both are quite evident. The M125A1 and M106A1 are currently in widespread service in the US Army, Reserves and National Guard. There are about 800 mortar carriers in the US Army, with additional vehicles in National Guard service. There are no plans currently to replace these vehicles as carriers with the new M2 chassis, but the mortar carriers will undoubtedly undergo improvements comparable to the newer M113A2 and M113A3 models. Some work has been done on mounting the 107mm mortar on a stretched M113 chassis, but there is currently no commitment from the Army to proceed in this direction. Other armies have used the M113 chassis for their own designs.

MECHANIZED FLAME-THROWERS

The M67. Flame-thrower teams are deployed mainly against fortified positions, and there are evident advantages to using an armoured vehicle to transport and protect the flame weapon. During the Second World War, various tracked vehicles were used as mechanized flame-throwers in a number of different configurations, especially the M5A1 Stuart and the M4 Sherman. These were used most extensively in the Pacific campaigns. The Sherman-based flame-throwers remained the standard type after the war, though new types were investigated. A fully armoured version of the M39 utility vehicle, the T65, was tested in 1953 and another version was tested on the M47 tank in 1955. Both were discarded in favour of a flame-thrower version of the M48. This vehicle, the M67, mounted an M7−6 flame-thrower in place of the vehicle's usual gun armament. The vehicle has a large 378-gallon fuel tank stowed, together with pressure tanks, in the turret. The flame-thrower has enough fuel to fire for 60 seconds

continuously, though the usual method is to fire bursts of several seconds' duration. The range of this weapon is 180 to 200 metres, though it depends on whether thickened or unthickened fuel is used. Production of 74 M67s for the Marines began in 1955, using the M48 as the basic chassis. In 1963 it was decided to mount them on the improved M48A2 chassis, and they were redesignated M67A1. The M67A1 was used in Vietnam to destroy bunkers.

The M132. The Army was reluctant to commit expensive main battle tanks to flame-thrower operations and developed a modified version of the Marine flame-thrower for mounting in a modified M113 APC. The fuel was stored in the troop compartment at the rear, and a small cupola was fitted with a flame-thrower tube and a coaxial 7.62mm machine-gun. These were accepted for service use as the M132 self-propelled flame-thrower; 201 were produced in 1964. In the meantime, kits for the M10−8 flame-thrower had been sent to Vietnam for trials, and modified vehicles were used there for the first time in 1963. The M132 carries 200 gallons of fuel and has a fire duration of 32 seconds continuously at a range of 150 to 170 metres. The M132s were usually deployed in three different units: a section-sized team, with three vehicles and accompanying service units to support a battalion; a platoon-sized team, also with three flame-throwers but heavier logistical support adequate to accompany a brigade-sized force; and a chemical, mechanized flame company with twelve M132, for support of a divisional-sized unit. The M132s were extensively used in Vietnam by both the US and ARVN forces, and were popularly called 'Zippos' by the troops after the well known cigarette lighter. Besides their use in a combat rôle, they were also used for defoliation around camp perimeters. The M132 is an M113 with the flame-thrower kit added, while the M132A1 is a factory-built vehicle with the flame-thrower already installed. An armoured version of the M548 tractor, the XM45E1, was used experimentally in Vietnam as a service vehicle for the M132.

There has been little further development of flame weapons, as the current types have proved adequate for combat use. In the early 1970s, the Army and Marines examined the feasibility of flame projectiles that could be fired from ordinary gun barrels as part of the FLASH programme, but these were not adopted for service use.

Left: Externally, the M132 mechanized flame-thrower is identical to the M113 armoured personnel carrier on which it is based, except for the flame-thrower turret assembly on the roof, shown in close-up here. Beside the flame tube is a coaxial .30 calibre machine-gun, though in this particular case the machine-gun is not installed. Behind the turret is a shielded .30 calibre machine-gun common on ARVN M132s. (James Loop)

Below: An Army M67A1 flame-thrower being demonstrated at Fort Knox in 1961. The M67 is used mainly by the Marines, and this particular version is based on the M48A2 Patton tank chassis. The main gun is replaced by a flame-thrower, but the flame-thrower tube is dummied to resemble the usual gun barrel so that the flame tank and its flammable cargo do not attract undue enemy attention. (US Army)

Right, top: Although there was no air opposition to contend with in Vietnam, the M42A1 Duster was a common sight on convoy escort duties and perimeter defence. This Duster took part in Operation 'Greely' in Dak To Province, July 1967. (US Army)

Right, below: The M42 Duster combined the twin 40mm Bofors anti-aircraft gun arrangement of the earlier M19 with a newer chassis closely derived from the M41 Walker Bulldog light tank. Although introduced into service in the early 1950s, small numbers of M42s still soldier-on in Reserve and National Guard units. This M42, wearing an intricate winter camouflage scheme, was used in support of the 23rd Infantry during the 'Willow Freeze' manoeuvres in Alaska in January 1961, which tested the suitability of armoured equipment in an Arctic environment. (US Army)

MECHANIZED ARTILLERY

Designation:	M44A1	M52A1	M53	M55	M108	M109	M109A2	M107	M110	M110A2	M106A1	M125A1	XM993
Production:	608	684			1,000	4,000 +				750			3
Crew:	5	5	6	6	5	6	6	5 + 7	5 + 7	5 + 7	6	6	3
Combat weight (kg):	29,030	24,040	43,545	44,452	21,274	23,796	24,811	28,168	26,535	28,350	11,848	11,067	22,680
Length overall (cm):	616	580	1,021	790	611	661	904	1,130	748	1,104	486	486	697
Length of hull (cm):	616	580	691	691	611	611	611	646	646	646	486	486	697
Height (cm):	311	331	356	356	330	330	330	315	315	315	250	250	259
Width (cm):	324	315	358	358	316	316	316	347	347	347	286	286	297
Main armament:	155mm M45	105mm M49	155mm M46	203mm M47	105mm M103	155mm M126	155mm M185	175mm M113	203mm M2A1	203mm M201	107mm M30	81mm M29	227mm rockets (12)
Weapon performance													
Round (type):	M107(HE)	M1(HE)	M107(HE)	M106(HE)	M1(HE)	M107(HE)	M549(HERA)	M437(HE)	M106(HE)	M650(HERA)	M3(HE)	M56(HE)	M42 (submunition HE)
Max. range (km):	9.7	11.27	23.5	16.9	11.5	14.6	24.0	32.7	16.8	30 +	3.9	3.6	30 +
Projectile weight (kg):	42.9	18.1	42.9	92.5	18.1	42.9	43.5	66.7	92.5	90	11.1	5.2	—
Elevation:	−5 +65°	−10 +65°	−5 +65°	−5 +65°	−4 +74°	−3 +75°	−3 +75°	−2 +65°	−2 +65°	−2 +65°	+45 +60°	+40 +80°	+60°
Rounds stowed:	24	105	20	10	87	28	36	2	2	2	88	114	12
Engine:	AOS1 895-5	AOS1 895-5	AV 1790-5B	AV 1790-5B	8V71T	8V71T	8V71T	8V71T	8V71T	8V71T	6V53	6V53	VTA − 903
Power to weight ratio (bhp/tonne):	17.24	20.8	16.2	15.8	18.03	17.02	16.3	14.37	15.26	14.37	16.6	16.6	22.0
Horsepower (bhp@rpm):	500@2,800	500@2,800	704@2,800	704@2,800	405@2,300	405@2,300	405@2,300	405@2,300	405@2,300	405@2,300	202@2,800	202@2,800	500
Max. road speed (km/hr):	56	67	48	48	56	56	56	55	55	55	64	64	64
Max. range:	122	161	257	257	386	390	354	724	724	724	483	483	483
Ground pressure (kg/cm^2):	.69	.62	.82	.82	.74	.79	.82	.81	.76	.81	.58	.55	.63

Mechanized Air Defence

SELF-PROPELLED AA GUNS

During the Second World War the US Army deployed a wide range of self-propelled anti-aircraft vehicles to defend motorized columns from air attack. In spite of the effort devoted to these vehicles, Allied air superiority over Europe and in the Pacific relieved the ground forces from frequent air attack, and as often as not the air defence vehicles were unused or committed to action against ground targets. The majority of these vehicles were based on the M3 half-track, and consisted of low-altitude weapons using twin or quad .50 calibre M2 machine-guns, such as the M16, or medium-altitude weapons, such as the M15 family, armed with twin .50 calibre machine-guns and a 37mm cannon. Both these classes of anti-aircraft weapons depended on optical sights for target acquisition and tracking. At the conclusion of the war, the Army was developing two very lethal anti-aircraft gun vehicles on the M24

tank chassis, a quad mounted .50 calibre in an armoured turret, and a twin 40mm Bofors in an exposed turret. The former offered few advantages over the M16 half-track, except for armour, and was not accepted for use. The latter was one of the most powerful self-propelled anti-aircraft weapons developed during the war. It entered production in 1945 as the M19 self-propelled 40mm gun but came too late to see combat. It was used in Korea, though, as was found in the Second World War, the lack of aircraft targets meant that it was used mainly as a ground defence weapon.

The main drawback to all these weapons was that their optical tracking layouts were only suitable for slow-flying aircraft at very low altitudes. The major advance in aircraft technology brought about by the jet engine outpaced air defence systems for use on a tracked chassis. The US Air Force had begun developing gun fire control radars for use on heavy

bombers, and so it was decided to attempt to integrate this technology with tracked air defence weapons. Using a modified T41 chassis, the T100 Stinger was designed and armed with quad .60 calibre (15mm) machine-guns. The Stinger used a fire control radar developed by Sperry Gyroscope and was ready for trials in 1952. In the meantime, it was decided to proceed with a vehicle with heavier firepower, the T141, which mounted the same twin 40mm gun assembly used on the M19 on an M41 chassis. The T53 Fire Control Carrier, which mounted the fire control radar to direct the T141, was designed at the same time. Both of these projects proved too costly and too complex, and would have required expensive and prolonged development. In 1952, the T141/T53 programme was cancelled, followed by the Stinger programme in 1955. However, the basic T141 vehicle was found to be an improvement over the M19, and was authorized for production as the M42 self-propelled twin 40mm gun.

The M42 Duster. The M42 basically consisted of a modified M41 chassis with the turret assembly from the older M19. In contrast to the M19, the M42 had the turret mounted in the centre of the vehicle instead of at the rear. Production continued through 1956 when an improved version with a fuel injection engine was introduced as the M42A1. The M42 is armed with two 40mm Bofors guns and has a maximum range of about 6 kilometres and a rate of fire of 240 rounds per minute. It uses conventional optical sights. The M42 and M42A1 were produced in large numbers in 1957, with a total of about 3,700 being manufactured. It was supplied to several NATO countries and proved a durable and useful anti-aircraft weapon. In view of the surprisingly slow development of Soviet ground-attack aircraft, it remained an adequate air defence weapon into the 1960s. The first combat use of the M42 with the Jordanian Army in 1967 was undistinguished. In 1966, two M42 battalions were sent to Vietnam. In view of the lack of any hostile air action, the M42A1s, popularly called Dusters, were used exclusively in the ground fire rôle. They were employed both for base security and perimeter defence, and for mobile convoy escort missions. Their heavy firepower made them very satisfactory in both capacities. Since 1968, the M42A1 was gradually phased out of service in the Regular Army, though about 470 still remain in service with the National Guard. The M42 also saw combat during the Lebanese Civil War. Several rudimentary fire control radars were developed by Lockheed and Sperry for the M42, but were not standardized in the US Army.

After the failure of the T100 Stinger programme, further studies were undertaken to determine whether a less complex fire control system and a twin 37mm armament might not result in a more functional weapon. In 1956, Sperry was contracted to begin work on a new self-propelled anti-aircraft gun, and a towed version was also initiated. In this case, the chassis was developed from M113 components, and the twin 37mm armament was dropped in favour of a General Electric 37mm Gatling gun. The first set of trials took place in 1960 and the vehicle was called the T249 Vigilante-B. The programme ran into trouble over the fire control system, the new gun and the overall complexity and cost of the weapon, and production was never contemplated. Interestingly enough, the Vigilante-B

was resurrected nearly a decade later in an improved form as a possible contender in the later Divisional Air Defence (DIVAD) programme.

By 1960, anti-aircraft missiles had begun to supplement air-defence guns for mobile anti-aircraft protection. The adoption by the US Army of the towed Hawk missile battery marked a major step forward in air defence, though the Hawk was still not mobile enough to accompany mechanized columns during the march. In 1959, the Army began a very ambitious programme to develop a smaller missile that could be carried in battery on a single, tracked vehicle with all associated fire control radars. This weapon was called the Mauler and was mounted on a modified M113, the XM546. The XM546 Mauler system consisted of the basic carrier with a launch array of twelve missiles mounted on the roof together with Raytheon tracking and acquisition radars developed from the Hawk programme. The missiles could be readily reloaded by a two-man crew. It was soon evident when the Mauler began trials that the requirements had pushed the existing technology a bit farther than was manageable. The system required too much equipment to be packaged into too small a vehicle, resulting in build-ups of high levels of heat and other problems. The missile was reportedly designed to engage targets as close as 500 metres, but was unstable at short ranges. Funding was heavily cut in 1964, and the programme was abandoned.

Both the Vigilante and Mauler programmes had attempted to develop extremely sophisticated weapons that were marginally beyond the technology of the time, and considerably beyond realistic cost, especially in view of the expanding costs of the Vietnam War. While development might have continued in less strained times, budget tightening and severe technical problems doomed both efforts. In their place, the Army decided to proceed with two low-risk stop-gaps, the Vulcan Air Defence System (VADS) and the Chaparral.

The M163 Vulcan. The Vulcan Air Defence System began in 1964 and included both a towed and tracked weapon. The aim was to develop a fire control system for the 20mm General Electric M61 Gatling gun. The tracked version of the system entered trials in 1965 and production began in 1967. The first systems were officially accepted by the Army in 1968 as the M163. The M163 basically consists of a modified M113, the M741, which differs from the troop carrier version in the configuration of the roof and troop compartment as well as in provisions for a suspension lockout system which is used when the gun is firing. Due to the heavier weight of the gun assembly, flotation cells are added to the hull sides and front to enable the M163 to remain amphibious. The M61A1 Vulcan gun is a derivative of the six-barrelled Gatling gun used on jet aircraft such as the F—104 Starfighter. It can fire at rates of 1,000 rounds per minute, and 3,000 rounds per minute or, in other words, up to 50 rounds a second. The vehicle carries 1,900 rounds of ammunition in containers within the hull; due to the prodigious consumption of ammunition by the gun, the weapon is fitted with a selector which allows the gunner to fire 10-, 30-, 60- or 100-round bursts. The guidance system consists of a VPS—2 range-only radar, an IFF unit and a stabilized lead computing sight. The turret is electrically traversed and elevated. The sighting system requires about one second to track the target before the lead is computed for the sight and then the system is ready to fire. Five M163s were rushed to Vietnam for trials in 1968, where they were employed mainly for convoy escort duty. They have seen combat use with the Israeli Army and with the Moroccan Army in the war with the Polisario guerrillas.

The M163 was accepted for production as a stop-gap with only modest performance, and was not entirely suitable for use against modern jet attack aircraft. Moreover, it was deployed in spite of the fact that it had reliability problems, and its accuracy was considered doubtful by many in the Army. As a result, a panel review was conducted in 1974 to examine ways of improving its performance. Several fire control radar systems were developed, but in

Left, top: The T249 Vigilante was an attempt to develop a more sophisticated replacement for the M42 Duster, with full radar fire direction and a 37mm Gatling automatic cannon. The project proved too complex and was abandoned. This pilot model, shorn of the sighting blister and radar, remains at Aberdeen Proving Grounds. (Steven Zaloga)

Left, middle: The M163 was a stop-gap attempt to fulfil the need for a short-range self-propelled air defence vehicle. The first M163 Vulcan were hastily shipped to Vietnam for combat trials, where they were used mainly for convoy escort. This particular M163 was part of the initial test unit in Vietnam, where they were photographed by one of the authors at Binh Long in December 1968. The following month this vehicle and the rest of the unit were involved in a convoy ambush on Highway 13 near Quan Lui, in which Lt. Harold Fritz of the 1/11th Armored Cavalry won the Medal of Honor for his part in fighting off the enemy attack. (James Loop)

Left, below: An M163 Vulcan provides air cover for a Canadian Centurion unit as part of Blue Force during the 1973 'Reforger IV' exercise. This Vulcan belonged to the 2/59th Air Defense of the 1st Armored Division. (US Army)

Below: An M163A1 Vulcan of the 1/55th Air Defense remains concealed in a stand of pine trees during the 1978 'Reforger' exercise at Fort Polk, Louisiana. The bow vane on the M163 had a flotation cell added to compensate for the weight of the Vulcan mount which allows the vehicle to swim across lakes or rivers. Flotation cells were also added to the hull side. (US Army)

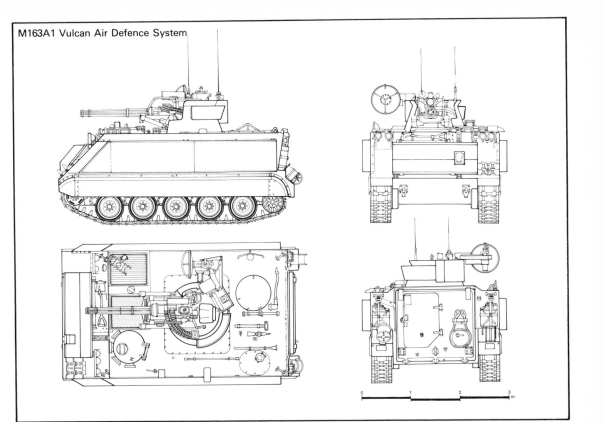

M163A1 Vulcan Air Defence System

1976 a long-term study of Army air defence needs concluded that the Vulcan's performance had so many shortcomings that a whole new system was warranted. The Army decided to fund new air defence weapons rather than try to improve the M163. The studies revealed that the M163 had only a thirteen per cent probability of downing a non-manoeuvring target flying at 250 knots, and against a jet flying at 450 knots its probability fell to a paltry five per cent. Moreover, since it was equipped with a ranging radar, it was effectively only a fair-weather, daylight system. These problems were all the more troubling when compared with the capabilities of the Soviet ZSU−23−4 Shilka, which had been introduced at about the same time and yet was an all-weather radar-directed weapon with far better lethality, as demonstrated in the 1973 Arab-Israeli War. The M163A1 has an upgraded radar.

The Divisional Air Defence (DIVAD) System. To begin the new effort, the Army funded Ford Aerospace to develop a test bed vehicle, the Gun Low Altitude Air Defence unit (or GLAAD), to examine various fire control options. The results of this test, conducted using twin 25mm dual-feed guns mounted on an MICV−65 (XM701) hull, concluded that a heavier calibre weapon with full radar-directed fire control backed up by new electro-optical sights was both feasible and desirable. In

1977, the Army asked for proposals from industry to meet these design goals. Emphasis was placed on commonality with existing NATO weapons and, to speed-up the process, it was decided to use a re-manufactured M48A5 Patton hull (XM988). Two firms, Ford Aerospace and General Dynamics, were selected to competitively develop the new DIVAD system (Divisional Air Defence).

The General Dynamics vehicle is based around a pair of twin Oerlikon KDA 35mm cannons as used in the German Gepard. The cannons are provided with dual-feed loading and have a combined fire rate of 1,100 rounds per minute in an automatic mode. There are 600 rounds carried in bins on either side of the turret. The gun has been designed to fire a wide range of ammunition, but the basic rounds would be a high-explosive incendiary and an armour-piercing discarding sabot round with tracer. The vehicle has a three-man crew, with two in the turret, a commander and gunner, and a driver in the hull. The fire controls are based around a search-while-track radar closely derived from the existing Navy Phalanx system. There are separate search-and-track antennas with a digital radar processor that offers automatic target acquisition, hostile aircraft identification, prioritization of targets, and direction during engagement. While the gun could be fired under complete radar direction, a redundant electro-

optical day/night stabilized sight with laser rangefinder was provided in case of battle damage or radar failure. The guns were electro-hydraulically elevated and traversed, and the crew was completely segregated from the weapons to avoid fume contamination of the crew compartment. The Ford entry was configured very similarly to the General Dynamics vehicle, but based around a pair of twin Bofors L/70 40mm guns and a search-and-track radar system derived from the Westinghouse unit in the F−16 fighter. The Ford entry also was equipped with a redundant electro-optical guidance system, and carries 698 ready rounds.

Both entries were designed to allow fire-on-the-move from the main guns, and incorporate recent advances in radar technology, such as low-pulse repetition waveform to offer precise range determination against low-flying helicopters, and multiple-beam tracking techniques to allow the guns to engage helicopters performing nap-of-the-earth evasion manoeuvres. The emphasis of the programme on the use of mature, existing sub-systems speeded along development immeasurably, and the two vehicles were competitively tested in 1980 with the Ford Aerospace entry being selected. The Army plans to purchase 618 XM988 DIVADs, which will completely replace the M163 except in the National Guard.

Left: The XM988 DIVAD developed by Ford Aerospace won the Army's contract for a new self-propelled air defence gun system in 1981. It is armed with twin 40mm Bofors guns, and the fire control radar is derived from the type used on the F–16 fighter. (Ford Aerospace)

Top: This mock-up of General Dynamics' DIVAD entry clearly shows the twin 35mm Oerlikon armament, and the acquisition and tracking radar domes. The electro-optical tracking sight is evident at the forward right-hand corner of the turret. (General Dynamics)

Middle: There have been several attempts to develop an air defence version of the M548 cargo carrier. The US Army experimentally mounted a twin 40mm gun assembly similar to that used on the M42 under the designation XM177, but this project was eventually dropped. In the late 1970s, Ares developed the Eagle air defence system (pictured here), which mounts twin 35mm guns, for a client in the Middle East, but export permission was refused by Congress. The Eagle ADS uses a remotely-positioned electro-optical tracking system for fire direction. (Ares Inc.)

Below: Among the many variants of the V–150 Commando series is an air defence model equipped with a 20mm Vulcan automatic cannon. This turret is based on the M167 wheeled Vulcan, which differs from the Vulcan used on the M163 in that the main ammunition tray is carried on the turret itself rather than being positioned in the hull. (Cadillac Gage)

MECHANIZED AIR DEFENCE

Self-Propelled AA Guns

Designation:	M42A1	M163	XM988[1]
Name:	Duster	Vulcan	DIVAD
Production:	3,700	3,800	618[2]
Crew:	6	4	3
Combat weight (kg):	22,453	12,310	48,000
Length overall (cm):	635	486	907
Width (cm):	323	285	363
Height (cm):	284	273	381
Base vehicle:	mod. M41	M113 (M741)	M48 (XM988)
Main armament:	twin 40mm M2A1	M168 20mm	twin 40mm
Rounds stowed:	480	1,900	698
Rate of fire (rpm):	240	3,000	240
Max. range/altitude (m):	9,475/5,000	2,200/1,200	9,000/5,000+
Guidance:	optical	lead computing range only	radar or optical
Radar:	no		full radar direction
Engine:	AOS1 895-5	6V53	AVDS 1790-2A
Horsepower (bhp@ rpm):	500@2,800	215@2,800	750@2,400
Power to weight ratio (bhp/tonne):	22.3	17.4	15.9
Max. road speed (km/hr):	72	68	50
Max. range (km):	161	483	494
Ground pressure (kg/cm²):	.65	.61	.83

Notes: [1] Data provisional. [2] Anticipated initial contract order.

SELF-PROPELLED AA MISSILES

The M48 Chaparral. After the failure of Vigilante and Mauler, the two low risk stop-gap systems to replace these were Vulcan and Chaparral. The Chaparral was a straightforward adaptation of the highly successful Sidewinder air-to-air missile. It consisted of a modified M548 cargo carrier (based on the M113), called the M730, mounting a removable missile launch station with four MIM–72 missiles. The launch station is mounted on a telescoping base, which is lowered when the vehicle is travelling and extended upward for firing. The station can be traversed through 360° and is operated by a single crewman. When in operation, the canvas cab hood and windshield are folded down and covered by blast plates. The launch system, consisting of the M730 vehicle and M54 launch station is designated the M48. While the individual Chaparral launchers are not equipped with radar, the composite Vulcan/Chaparral battalions, each with twenty-four M163s and twenty-four Chaparrals, are provided with an MPQ–39 FAAR (Forward Area Alerting Radar) which informs the vehicles when targets are approaching. The targets are then optically acquired and the MIM–72s launched. The MIM–72 uses an infra-red seeking guidance system that homes in on the radiant heat from the aircraft target. Several improvements have

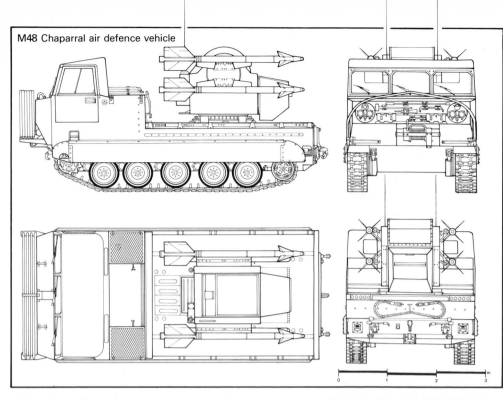

M48 Chaparral air defence vehicle

been made on the MIM – 72, notably the MIM – 72C which uses a new fuze and warhead. A further modified MIM – 72 will be introduced which uses a smokeless engine and an improved guidance system with a sophisticated IR/UV rosette scan technique. The M48 is currently a daytime-only system, but a modification programme began in 1980 to fit the launch station with a thermal imaging FLIR sight to allow use of the system at night. Consideration had been given to a more elaborate radar direction system, but in view of the cost and the expected arrival of the newer Roland system, the FLIR was felt to be more cost effective.

The XM975 Roland. It was evident from the outset that the Chaparral had many limitations, but it was adopted until a more satisfactory short-range system could be developed. The US Army was less concerned than the Soviet Army over the development of mobile air defence weapons, for the simple reason that NATO tactical strike aircraft were far more numerous and capable than Warsaw Pact forces, and only recently with the arrival of the MiG – 27 and later model Sukhois has the Warsaw Pact begun to approach the sophistication of the NATO allies in ground-attack aircraft. To handle these new threats, the Euromissile consortium decided to develop the Roland II to engage fast-moving targets within a 5 – 6.5 kilometre envelope. The US Army evaluated the Roland alongside the Rapier system in 1975 and decided to adopt the Roland. To provide mobility for the Roland launch assembly, a modified M109 SP howitzer chassis was chosen, designated the XM975. The fire unit assembly to be mounted on this vehicle will be manufactured in the United States, as will the XMIM – 115 missiles.

The American version of the Roland underwent tests in 1979 that uncovered many difficulties and prompted Congressional criticism. Many of the problems stemmed from misunderstandings between the Franco-German Euromissile consortium and their American counterparts, but eventually the problems were resolved. Production began in 1979, and the current Army plans call for ninety-five fire units. This total was a reduction on earlier figures owing to a Department of Defense decision to buy instead Rapier missiles for defending air bases in Britain. The Rolands will serve in divisional air defence battalions with twelve XM975 Rolands and thirty-six XM988 DIVADs, or in independent battalions with thirty-six Rolands.

The Roland uses a three-man crew consisting of a commander, driver and radar operator. The XM993 carries two missiles on the launchers with eight spares contained immediately below in the hull. The Roland system automatically reloads after firing, in contrast to the Chaparral which is manually reloaded. The surveillance radar, located atop the traversable firing assembly, is a low-frequency band pulse doppler type which scans at one revolution per

Self-Propelled AA Missiles		
Designation:	M48	XM975[1]
Name:	Chaparral	Roland
Production:		95[2]
Crew:	6	3-4
Combat weight (kg):	12,600	26,000
Length overall (cm):	609	737
Width (cm):	269	316
Height (cm):	289	461
Base vehicle:	M548 (M730)	M109 (XM975)
Missile:	MIM – 72 Chaparral	Roland II
Rounds stowed:	4 + 8	2 + 8
Number of launchers:	4	2
Reloading:	manual	automatic
Effective range/altitude (m):	5,000/3,000	6,000 + /5,000 +
Missile guidance:	IR homing	IR/microwave command guidance
Target acquisition:	optical	radar or optical
Radar:	no	acquisition and tracking
Engine:	6V53	8V71T
Horsepower (bhp@rpm):	215@2,800	405@2,300
Power to weight ratio (bhp/tonne):	17.3	15.5
Max. road speed (km/hr):	61	54
Max. range (km):	504	320
Ground pressure (kg/cm²):	.59	.85

Notes: [1] Provisional data. [2] Anticipated initial contract batch for US Army only.

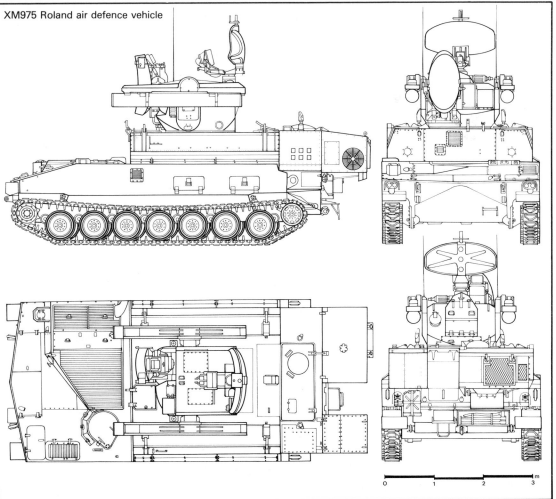

XM975 Roland air defence vehicle

Left, middle: The failure of the Mauler programme led the Army to develop a stop-gap system, the Chaparral, which is based around the highly successful Sidewinder air-to-air missile. An array of four launchers was mounted on a modified M548 cargo carrier chassis, called the M730 in this configuration. This view shows a Chaparral launcher of the Israeli Army with the launch assembly folded for travel and protective covers over the seeker heads of the MIM – 72 missiles. (Israeli Defence Force)

Left, below: The Chaparral missile launch assembly is elevated hydraulically when in the firing mode, and the cab vacated and covered by blast plates. The large bars at the front of the vehicle are hoops for the tarpaulin that covers the back bed of the vehicle during long journeys. In the background is an Israeli Army M163 Vulcan. (Israeli Defence Force)

Above: The US Army decided to adopt the Franco-German Roland to satisfy the need for a sophisticated low-altitude air defence missile to protect mechanized formations. The Roland will be manufactured in the United States and mounted on a modified version of the M109 chassis, called the XM975. The vehicle incorporates both a tracking and acquisition radar, and an electro-optical sight, all mounted in the small turret at the top of the vehicle. The missile launcher is automatically reloaded from storage containers at the side of the vehicle underneath the launcher. (Hughes Aircraft Co.)

second and is capable of acquiring helicopters and other extremely low-flying aircraft. The system has a range of about eighteen kilometres, and fixed echoes are suppressed to ease the work of the operator. When a target is acquired, it is interrogated by an IFF unit and, if judged hostile, comes under the coverage of either the optical tracking sight or the tracking radar. The tracking radar is a two-channel monopulse high frequency band type, with one channel used to maintain the target while the other links up with a microwave source on the missile to measure its deviation from the correct trajectory to hit the target. Once the target has been acquired, the decision is made to engage. Either the optical sight or tracking radar can be used to guide the missile; in clear weather during

daylight the optical sight is preferred due to its slightly better accuracy. Should the optical mode be chosen, on launch of the missile an infra-red tracker locks-on to an infra-red transmitter located at the rear of the missile and transmits course information to the command computer, which in turn transmits corrections to the missile in a high frequency band with varying frequencies and selectable pulse codes to resist jamming attempts. In the radar mode, the tracking radar acquires signals from a microwave transmitter at the tail of the missile which it uses to determine corrections beamed by the command computer's transmitter. It is possible to switch from radar to optical mode or vice versa even during the course of a missile launch. All ten missiles can be fired in a few minutes.

One of the most radical approaches to air defence was undertaken by the Army's MTU (Mobile Test Unit) in 1976. The Mobile Test Unit is a prototype LVT-7 modified to carry a laser weapon, power generator and a beam pointing and tracking system. The laser weapon is a high energy electric discharge laser which punctures a hole in its target by a beam of intense, coherent light. The MTU was not envisaged as a prototype air defence weapon since the power levels of the available lasers were much too low to be effective. It did manage to shoot down several drones during trials, but its performance is inadequate against modern attack aircraft. Nevertheless, it may serve as a forerunner to a beam air defence weapon once laser weapon technology has matured sufficiently.

Top left: Among the most ambitious air defence projects undertaken by the Army in the 1960s was the ill-fated Mauler programme. This system was designed to incorporate the full missile array, as well as tracking and acquisition radar, on a single vehicle derived from the M113 APC, but proved too complex for existing technology (US Army)

Top right: A fully-tracked version of the highly successful Hawk missile launcher was developed in the late 1960s and called the M727. Each tracked carrier, derived from the M548 cargo carrier, mounted three Hawk missiles and towed a part of the Hawk battery tracking and acquisition radar. This configuration was not as successful as the standard towed Hawk battery, and was eventually phased out. These M727 served with the 32nd Air Defense Command during 'Reforger II' and are seen crossing a Mobile Floating Assault Bridge over the Main River in Germany on 19 October 1970. (US Army)

Left: Among the most radical air defence vehicles developed by the Army in the 1970s was the experimental MTU, based on the LVT-7. This mounted an electric discharge laser, which was successfully test-fired against drones. Laser technology is not yet mature enough to enable a weapon to be deployed, but the MTU stands as a primitive precursor to these weapons. (US Army)